Nagel / Huether

Nagel / Huether

By David Emmick

The flying A

Flying A Books
Issaquah, Washington

Nagel / Huether

Flying A books may be ordered through lulu.com

Flying A Books
Issaquah, Washington

ISBN: 978-1-304-73506-5

Printed in the United States of America

Montani Semper Liberi

Mountaineers Forever Free

Contents

Preface

This is the story of the Nagel and Huether families. This is my mother Edna's family. She was born into a large family with many brothers and sisters. Her father was John Nagel and her mother was Barbara. Her father John Nagel was a German from Russia but we don't know much about him. Barbara's father was Paul Huether who was also a German from Russia. His father was also named Paul Huether.

You may find that I've repeated the same information over several times. As I did research I found that I needed more context and I've tried to provide this same context to the reader so it's easier to tell who is who and who is related to who.

I'm sure as time goes by there will be revisions to this book and stories to add. Consider this a work in progress that will be updated from time to time. Enjoy.

-David

Chapter 1 – Family Origins

My mother **Edna Ottile NAGEL** was born October 12, 1925 in Lind, Washington to John and Barbara Nagel. Barbara's maiden name was Huether. We know little about her father's family but he was said to be a relative of the Huethers, possibly a forth cousin, and they may have been in Russia at the same time. "Nagel" means nail smith in German; it may also be spelled Nogel.

The Huether family is better documented. *Spelled Huether; Pronounced: "Hee-Thur" or "Hee-Ter".* Since we know little about the Nagel family we will concentrate on the Huether family and use Edna's mother Barbara [Huether] Nagel as the focus of Huether ancestry relating the various family members to her for clarity.

Paul Huether Jr.'s sister (**Barbara's** aunt) Maria Barbara Huether married Gottlob Hochstatter in Russia. They immigrated to the United States through Canada and moved to South Dakota. After staying with relatives they moved to Washington State near Black Lake in October of 1902 where they homesteaded 170 acres near Wilson Creek (filed 1903) and about 10 miles northeast of Moses Lake. Gottlob and Marie's daughter Barbara married Jakob Ottmar. The Ottmar land is located about 12 miles south of the Hochstatter land (Paul Sr. and Paul Jr. are buried in the Ottmar Cemetery).

After the death of his second wife in 1905, Paul Huether Sr. (**Barbara's** grandfather) moved to the state of Washington to live with his daughter Maria Barbara who was married to Gottlob Hochstatter. Paul Jr.'s son Christ Huether (Barbara's brother) homesteaded 86 acres of land (patent 1920) about 15 miles southeast of the Hochstatter's land.[1] In 1908 Paul Sr. bought 160 acres of land near Rocky Coulee southeast of Ruff and about 12 miles

[1]Christ Huether Homestead, Grant County Final Receipt Vol. B pages 105-106

southeast of the Hochstatter's land and about 2 miles north of his grandson Christ's homestead.

In 1908 Paul Jr. and his family moved by wagon to Washington state to be with Paul's father Paul Sr. In the 1910 Grant County U.S. Census Paul Huether Jr. age 58 and Katherina age 41 are listed as living in Wheeler.[2] Living with Paul and Katherina are son Henry age 20, daughters Caroline age 17, Margrette age 16, **Barbara** age 14, son Andrew age 13, daughter Lydia age 11, son Paul Jr. age 10, daughter Sophia age 8, daughters E. E. (Eva) age 6, and Adeline age 4 and son Jacob S. age 1 and 3 months.

John Nagel married **Barbara** Huether on March 15th, 1917 and settled near Lind on a purchased farm. He had been working on a nearby farm and was considered a good catch. Their daughter Edna (my mother) was born on the farm near Lind. When they lost the farm to a bad crop the family moved to Spangle, then Newman Lake and later to Rathdrum.

This is the story of the Huether and Nagel families as they settled in Washington and later in Idaho. The first several chapters cover the Huether ancestors. Family stories and old pictures are combined with legal documents and land descriptions as well as recent pictures of the lands they owned.

Ludwig Huether is the oldest known member of the Huether family. My mother is descended from Paul Sr. the sixth child of Ludwig.

Ludwig Huether and Barbara Zechmeister's place of birth are not known with certainty. Paul Huether's death certificate states they were born in Germany. The 1905 census of Paul Huether states his parents were born in Hungary. Some descendants indicate Ludwig and Barbara were born in Düsseldorf, Germany and immigrated to Hungary and then to Russia. Research indicates that Ludwig and Barbara emigrated to Petersdorf, near Odessa, Russia in the year 1805. They likely are Germans who migrated first to Hungary and then to Russia.

Peterstal was founded about 1800 when the general proclamation to would-be colonists was issued in the Kingdom of Hungary, where families from Wuerttemberg and the Rhineland had already been settled as farmers. Our ancestors decided to immigrate to Russia. They arrived near Odessa in the summer of 1805 and built themselves wattled huts of reed and grass.

---

[2]1910 U.S. CENSUS, Grant County, Washington; Page 270A, image file 0160.tif, Record ID HRP1910GRT5375

Stuttgart South of Frankfort

Düsseldorf Nordrhein-Westfalen, Northwest of Frankfort

Descendants of Ludwig HUETHER - First Generation

Family Tree First Generation

Ludwig HUETHER (1799 – 1940)
+ Maria Barbara ZECHMEISTER (1800-)
  Maria Barbara HUETHER (1823 – 1848)
  +Jacob PRIESTER (1821 -)
  Hanes HUETHER (1825 – 1868)
  Georg Nicolaus HUETHER (1827 – 1862)
  Georg Peter HUETHER (1827 – 1862)
  Ludwig HUETHER (1828 – 1907)
  Paul HUETHER Sr. (1830-1931)
  Eva Elisabetha HUETHER (1831 -)
  Elisabetha Margartha HUETHER (1833-1897)
  Georg Fredrich HUETHER (1834 – 1834)
  Rosina Catherine HUETHER (1836 – 1876)
  Elisabetha Gertrude HUETHER (1837 -)
  Simon HUETHER (1838 – 1914)
  Jakob HUETHER (1840-1896)

Ludwig Huether and Barbara Zechmeister likely immigrated to Hungary and then to Russia. They arrived near Odessa in the summer of 1805. We are descended from their sixth child Paul Huether Sr. It is Paul Sr. that immigrated to the United States first settling in North Dakota and then moving to Washington State.

1. **Johann Ludwig Jacob HUETHER** was born 7 May 1799 in Neu Verbes, Hungary. He died 29 Jul 1940 in Peterstal, Grossliebental, Ukraine, Russia. The name Hitter was found in Wien, in Dusenbach, in Bayers and in Lienzingen Minster. The German meaning of the name Hutter or Huter means a guard or watchman.
Ludwig married **Maria Barbara Margaretha ZECHMEITSTER**, daughter of Paul ZECHMEITSTER and Rosina BAMER, on 1823 in Peterstal, S. Russia. Barbara was born 28 May 1800 in Peterstal, S. Russia.
They had the following children:

2 F i **Maria Barbara HUETHER** was born 1 Nov 1823 in Peterstal, Russia. She died 19 Jul 1848 in Peterstal, S. Russia.
Maria married **Jacob PRIESTER** on 21 Nov 1844 in Peterstal, S. Russia. Jacob was born 28 Jul 1821 in Freudental.

3 M ii **Johannes Hanes HUETHER** "John" was born 21 Aug 1825 in Peterstal, S. Russia. He died 18 Nov 1868 in Berlin, S. Russia.

4 M iii **Johann Georg Nicolaus HUETHER** was born 27 Jan 1827 in Peterstal, S. Russia. He died 15 Oct 1862 in Peterstal, S. Russia.

5 M iv **Georg Peter HUETHER** was born 3 Apr 1827 in Peterstal, Odessa, South Russia. He died 1 Jan 1905 in Ukraine, S. Russia. twin to Ludwig.

6 M v **Ludwig HUETHER** was born 3 Apr 1828 in Peterstal, Russia. He died 28 Aug 1907 in Bridgewater, South Dakota. twin to Georg Nicolaus.

\+ 7 M vi **<u>Paul HUETHER Sr.</u>** was born 6 Feb 1830 and died 13 Mar 1931.

8 F vii **Eva Elisabetha HUETHER** was born 1 Sep 1831 in Peterstal, S. Russia.

9 F viii **Elisabetha Margartha HUETHER** "Elisagred" was born 26 Feb 1833 in Peterstal, S. Russia. She died 1897 in Eureka, South Dakota.

10 M ix **Georg Fredrich HUETHER** was born 18 Nov 1834 in Peterstal, S. Russia. He died 18 Nov 1834 in Peterstal, S. Russia.

11 F x **Rosina Catherine HUETHER** "Rose" was born 3 Mar 1836 in Peterstal, S. Russia. She died 22 Feb 1876 in Odessa, S. Russia. She never married. She was a private school teacher for a wealthy family in Odessa, Russia and taught German, Spanish and Russian. The Odessa City death records show her death date as Feb. 22, 1876 at Peterstal.

12 F xi **Elisabetha Gertruda HUETHER** "Gertrude" was born 15 Jun 1837 in Peterstal, S. Russia.

13 M xii **Simon HUETHER** was born 27 Dec 1838 in Peterstal, S.

Russia. He died 12 Feb 1914 in Parkston, South Dakota.

14 M xiii **Jakob HUETHER** was born 20 Apr 1840 in Peterstal, S. Russia. He died 10 Jun 1896.

Descendants of Ludwig HUETHER - Second Generation

Family Tree Second Generation

Paul HUETHER Sr. (1830-1931)
+Anna Margareta CRISTMAN (1852 – 1892)
  Paul HUETHER Jr. (1853 – 1918)
  Maria Barbara HUETHER (1854 – 1947)
  +Johann Gottlob HOCHSTETTER (1852 – 1918)
  ...
    Barbara HOCHSTATTER (1876 – 1968)
    +Jakob OTTMAR (1874 – 1954)
  ...
  Johannes HUETHER (1856 – 1858)
  Elizabetha HUETHER (1859-1932)
  Katherina HUETHER (1861-1946
  Ludwig HUETHER (1863-1932)
  Karoline HUETHER (1865 -)
  Margarethe HUETHER (1867-1963)
  Heinrich HUETHER (1868-1941)
  Simon HUETHER (1871 -)
  Edith Rosina HUETHER (1873 – 1940)
  Johann HUETHER (1874 – 1875)
  Lousia HUETHER (1878 – 1892)
+Louisa Christmann HETTICH (1833 – 1905)

Paul Sr. was the sixth child of Johann Ludwig Jacob Huether and Barbara Margareth Zechmeister. He was born 6 February 1830 in Peterstal and died in Eugene, Oregon. He is buried in an unmarked grave in the Ottmar cemetery. He married Maria (Anna) Margaretha Christmann on 25 May 1852 in Freudental, Russia. Paul was a shoemaker in Russia.

Paul is listed two places in the Peterstal Liebental District Odessa in the 1858 census. He is listed in house #23 as a member of Widow Barbara (Zechmeister) Huether's household and his own house #26 with his wife Margaretha and three children. Paul is also listed twice in the Peterstal Liebental District Odessa 1841-1860 Church Family Book. He is listed on page

73 with his wife and five children and page 85 as a member of his mother's family.

1905
Card No.
Sex
Color
Married
Single
Widowed ✓
Divorced
Read
Write
Blind Deaf
Insane Idiot
Naturalized?
Years in U. S. 13
Years in S. D. 13

Name Paul Huether Age 74
County Walworth P.O. Java
Town Ward
Occupation retired Own Home?
Birthplace Russia Ancestry
Father's birthplace Hungary
Mother's birthplace Hungary
Education Graduate of
War Service: Spanish World I World II
State Company Reg. Division
Maiden Name of wife
Church affiliation
Signed Assessor

Born — 1831

Taken from the Bureau of Census files 1905, Pierre, South Dakota

Paul and his two brothers, Ludwig and Simon, immigrated to the United States. Paul and his wife left Neusatz, South Russia, where they had moved in 1858 and immigrated to Menno, South Dakota in 1889 before going to Mound City, South Dakota where he homesteaded. They filed claims in Blessing Township, Campbell County, South Dakota.

Paul and his wife, Maria, had 14 children. My great grandfather was their first child named Paul after his father. The elder Paul Huether was married twice; there were no children by the second wife. Paul was one of the people instrumental in organizing the Odessa Reformed Church in Sutley, Campbell County, South Dakota. Paul is listed on the South Dakota 1900 Federal Census as living in Campbell County, Blessing Township.

After the death of his second wife, Louisa (Rosa) Christmann Hettich, in 1905, he moved to the state of Washington to live with family members. Paul's two brothers also homesteaded in South Dakota and remained there until they died.

Barbara Nagel's grandfather,
Paul Huether, born July 2, 1831 died Feb. 13, 1931

7. Paul HUETHER Sr. (Ludwig Jacob) was born 6 Feb 1830 in Peterstal, S. Russia. He died 13 Mar 1931 in Eugene, Oregon.
Paul was a shoemaker in Russia. Paul married Anna Margareta Christman. They were both Lutheran and changed to the Reform Church. When he was 74 he was a retired farmer. He left Neusatz where he had moved in 1858 near Odessa, S. Russia and immigrated in 1889 to Menno, South Dakota before going to Mound City, South Dakota where he homesteaded. They filed claims in Blessing Township, Campbell County, South Dakota.
Anna Margareta and her daughter Louise died that year in 1889 in Menno, S. Dakota. Paul married a second wife, a Hittich who died in 1908 at McLaughlin, South Dakota. Paul moved to Washington State in 1905.
This death date was from a certified copy from the Oregon State Board of Health vital Statistics Section that Elsie Huether received Nov. 20, 1969. He is buried in an unmarked grave in the Ottmar Cemetery near Moses Lake, Washington.
Paul married (1) Anna Margareta CHRISTMAN on 25 May 1852 in Freudental, S. Russia. Anna was born 12 Oct 1832 in Freudental, S. Russia. She died 4 Feb 1892 in Mound City, South Dakota.
They had the following children:

+ 15 M i Paul HUETHER Jr. was born 19 Jan 1853 and died 8 Sep 1918.

+ 16 F ii Maria Barbara HUETHER was born 24 Sep 1854 and died 10 Oct 1947. Maria married Johann Gottlob HOCHSTATTER and this family is detailed later. Their daughter Barbara married Jakob OTTMAR and this family is detailed later.

17 M iii Johannes HUETHER was born 20 Jun 1856 in Peterstal, S. Russia. He died 11 Jan 1858 in Helenental, S. Russia.

18 F iv Elisabetha HUETHER "Eliza" was born 1 Nov 1859 in Neusatz, S. Russia. She died 9 Apr 1932 in Siberia from starvation.

19 F v Katharina HUETHER was born 8 Apr 1861 in Neusatz, S. Russia. She died Sep 1946 in Odessa, Washington.

20 M vi Ludwig HUETHER was born 5 Jul 1863 in Neusatz, S. Russia. He died Jun 1932 in Twin Falls, ID.

21 F vii Karoline HUETHER was born 21 May 1865 in Neusatz, S. Russia.

22 F viii Margarethe HUETHER was born 24 Jun 1867 in Neusatz, S. Russia. She died 10 Jul 1963 in Bismark, North Dakota.

23 M ix Heinrich HUETHER "Henry" was born 17 Jun 1868 in Neusatz, S. Russia. He died 5 Sep 1941 in Ashley, North Dakota.

24 M x Simon HUETHER was born 20 Nov 1871 in Neusatz, S. Russia.

25 F xi Edith Rosina HUETHER "Rose" was born 27 Apr 1873 in Neusatz, S. Russia. She died Sep 1940 in Eugene, Oregon.

26 M xii Johann HUETHER was born 9 Sep 1874 in Neusatz, S. Russia. He died 25 Aug 1875 in Neusatz, S. Russia.

27 M xiii Christian HUETHER was born 22 Dec 1876 in Neusatz, S. Russia. He died 7 Aug 1959 in Los Angeles, CA.

28 F xiv Louisa HUETHER was born 1878 in Neusatz, S. Russia. She died Jan 1892 in Campbell County, South Dakota.

Paul also married (2) Louisa Christmann HETTICH "Rosa", daughter of Andrew HETTICH, about 1891. Rosa was born Jul 1833 in Russia. She died 8 Apr 1905 in McLaughlin, South Dakota.

Her daughter Louisa born October 1876 was still at home when the mother married Paul. One source has her death as March 14, 1905. Louisa (Rosa) is buried near McLaughlin, South Dakota.

Chapter 2 - Germans from Russia

Paul HUETHER (son of Paul, son of Ludwig) was born 19 January 1853 in Peterstal, South Russia.

Peterstal, Grossliebental, Ukraine, Russia near Odessa

Odessa, Ukraine

This is taken from Germans from Russia Heritage Collection
North Dakota University, Fargo, N.D.
http://library.ndsu.edu/grhc/history_culture/index.html

Gordon L. Iseminger is professor of history at the University of North Dakota. He obtained his undergraduate training at Augustana College and his graduate degrees from the University of South Dakota and the University of Oklahoma. A scholar of European and ethnic history, Iseminger has published articles and reviews in a variety of journals including North Dakota History. He is author of The Quartzite Border: Surveying and Marking the North Dakota - South Dakota Boundary, 1891-92 (1988).

The Germans from Russia

Wanting to protect her frontiers and learn the new advanced farming methods Russian Czarina Catherine the Great in 1762 offered German farmers land. Czarina Catherine was a former German princess. She promised colonists autonomy and farm land in Russia should they choose to emigrate. Catherine believed these highly skilled farmers and tradesmen would promote progress leading to a more modern Russia. Being demoralized from many years of

religious strife, political chaos and economic hardship many accepted her offer and colonized the Volga region first, to be known as the Volga Germans.
In 1804, Germans colonized the southern Ukraine (known as the Black Sea Germans). More emigrated from Württemberg and Prussia around 1812 and became the Bessarabian Germans.

In 1872, the Imperial Russian Government revoked colonists' privileges to begin Russification, caused by growing Slavic resentment toward these German foreigners. Treasuring their own identity and culture and seeking better opportunities elsewhere, many of the German Russians decided to leave. Those immigrating to North America settled throughout the Great Plains from Saskatchewan to Texas.

From Iseminger, Dr. Gordon. "Are we Germans, or Russians, or Americans?" North Dakota History 59, (1992) 2-16 and posted at Germans from Russia Heritage Collection
North Dakota University, Fargo, N.D.
http://library.ndsu.edu/grhc/history_culture/index.html

> To understand German-Russians is to appreciate their land hunger. Promised land, Germans from Baden, Bavaria, Württemberg, and the Palatinate had accepted the invitations of Catherine the Great and Alexander I to settle in south Russia. When asked by Works Progress Administration interviewers in the late 1930s why they had come to North Dakota, most German-Russians answered: "Land." Of the 217 German-Russians in McIntosh County old enough to declare an occupation in 1885, all but five - four men and one woman - were farmers who had taken up land. The four men were younger than twenty-one years of age and could not yet file on homesteads. The woman was unmarried and also under age.
> In 1890, 2,053 of the county's 3,248 inhabitants were German-Russians. Twenty years later, in 1910, McIntosh County contained 7,251 people, most of them of foreign stock. Of the total population, 5,745, nearly 80 percent, listed Russia as the birthplace of themselves or of their parents, that is, they were German-Russians.
> A common migration route followed by the Black Sea German-Russians who took up residence in McIntosh County was to travel from Odessa on the Black Sea to a German port such as Bremen by rail. Here they took ship passage across the Atlantic to New York and rail passage to Aberdeen, Ipswich, or Eureka in Dakota. Eureka, a relatively

small prairie town, was for many years a terminal for the Chicago, Milwaukee & St. Paul Railway and, despite its size, the world's leading primary wheat market. Eureka was also the main collecting and dispersal point for hundreds of German-Russian immigrants and, as "the Odessa of the Northern Great Plains," it "loomed larger than life in the consciousness of countless German-Russian emigrants." Odessa, Berlin, Johnstons, Lowell, Myrtle, Jewell, and Coldwater are the names of the seven townships, west to east, on the southern edge of McIntosh County. The total population of these seven townships in 1910 was 1,607. In every township, with the exception of Johnstons in which the village of Venturia was located, every person lived on a farm. By far the majority, 90 to 100 percent (the exception again being Johnstons), of the male heads of households were farmers.

The census listed a total of 458 parents in the seven townships. Of these, 390, or 85 percent, had been born in Russia. In no township were fewer than 70 percent of the parents born in Russia, and in most townships the figure was 90 percent or over. Even in Johnstons the figure was 82 percent, suggesting that some of the townspeople who had been born in Russia had chosen not to live on farms. Of the total of 458 parents in the seven townships, almost 75 percent listed German as their only language. Clearly, in 1910 the southern tier of townships in McIntosh County was decidedly rural and populated by German-Russians who had only recently arrived in North Dakota and who had not yet learned English.

…

German-Russian immigrants were also of peasant stock, but with this difference: Their ancestors had gone to South Russia determined to maintain their language, religion, and culture. As a consequence, they were an isolated people, a fact of incalculable significance. They took with them no educated Germans - pastors, priests, teachers, professionals, traders - and they lost virtually all contact with Germany. They were cut off from the remarkable progress that took place in Germany during the nineteenth century. Germans in South Russia were farmers. Few had the time, ability, money, or inclination to buy and read books and newspapers. Isolation and the lack of educated people among themselves were responsible for the lack of interest in schools and education in the German colonies in South Russia. Displaying more interest in religion than in education, they lavished far more money on their churches than they did on their schools. Even when German-language elementary schools were established in the colonies, the people continued to be more absorbed in farming than in education. Because the educated people among them - foreign priests and pastors, Russian officials, and traders - tricked and abused them, Germans in South Russia distrusted educated people and had little respect for them. The few German-Russian young people who received an education did so because they were weak and sickly and therefore considered unfit to make a living from the land.

German-Russians in North Dakota exhibited the same characteristics they had in Russia. They clung to their language, shunned contact with other nationalities, neglected schools, and disliked free public education and compulsory attendance laws. Few German-Russian children completed the eighth grade and it was unusual for a German-Russian young person to attend high school. Many German-Russian parents took it as a compliment when their children chose to help with farm work rather than spend their time reading or studying.

...

Although McIntosh County German-Russians had German blood in their veins, bore German names, and spoke German, it would be a mistake to confuse them with the Reichsdeutsche, or Empire Germans. German-Russians were known variously as "the Czar's Germans," because they had lived in Russia; or as North Dakota's "other Germans," because they had not been born in Germany and had never lived there. Timothy J. Kloberdanz suggested that a fitting designation for the "other Germans" is Volksdeutsche, a term that can be rendered not altogether satisfactorily in English as "ethnic Germans."

When contrasted to the Reichsdeutsche, German-Russians may have been akin to "stomach" Germans, Frederick C. Luebke's somewhat inelegant term for a group of German-Americans. "Stomach" Germans wanted to read the news in their German-language newspapers, drink their beer in the company of other Germans, use the German language in their worship services, and sing the old songs in their native tongue. Distinct from the stomach Germans, according to

Luebke, were the "soul" Germans. Convinced that German ideals and the German spirit were the noblest and loftiest in Western civilization and believing that they should be perpetuated in America, "soul" Germans idealized, articulated, and rationalized what they perceived to be their superior culture.

When German-Russians arrived in North Dakota, they suffered what Elwyn B. Robinson described as "a revolution in status." Signs of this impending revolution became evident as soon as the German-Russians boarded the ships that would take them to America. To their dismay, they discovered that there were very few differences between them and the peasants of other nationalities who were travelling with them. This was a bitter realization for Black Sea Germans who had come to regard themselves as belonging to a privileged class in Russia. In Russia they were leaders and in the upper social stratum. They had been admired by the Russian peasants and envied for their fine houses, productive farms, good horses, and sleek cattle. In North Dakota, they were at the other end of the social and economic scale. Other nationalities looked down on them, and many German-Russians complained that they were treated more condescendingly by the Reichsdeutsche than by any non-German speaking group. Having observed this phenomenon in western North Dakota, a Roman Catholic priest wrote: "To the average German, the German-Russian was an Ausländer. A literal translation of the word Ausländer would be "a person from outside the country," or, more briefly put, "a foreigner." Neither definition, however, does justice to the word as a German would use it with reference to a German-Russian. To fully appreciate the term's implications, one would have to include in the definition what an Englishman means when he uses the word "provincial," plus an "amused tolerance, veiled contempt, and a plentiful superiority."

Nor did the German-Russians identify with the Germany of the Reichsdeutsche. Their allegiance was to the Germany of the turn of the nineteenth century, to the Germany of the time of their Auswanderung, or emigration. German-Russians had not shared in the remarkable economic, industrial, scientific, and cultural advances that Germans had made in the nineteenth century. There were no '48ers among them. They did not identify with Prussian generals named

Moltke, and they took no vicarious pleasure in the Prussian victories over Austria and France on the battlefield. They did not swell with pride at mention of the Germany that Bismarck's policy of Blood and Iron had created in 1871. They had no affinity with William II's Weltpolitik, nor did they appreciate his desire to secure Germany's "place in the sun."

For the Reichsdeutsche, Germany was a distinct place - their historic homeland, their native land, their nation. To the German-Russians, however, Germany was "a deeply sentimental, even mystical, ... ancient Vaterland." And, despite their affection for the Fatherland, German-Russians had not hesitated to leave in search of better conditions. International borders and governments meant little to them; they knew that both changed frequently and quickly. It seemed, observed Kloberdanz, that the only Germany the German-Russians required was "a personalized one carried deep within."

Although German-Russians shared blood, language, narratives, proverbs, folk songs, and religious faith with Germans from Germany, they were different from them. And the Reichsdeutsche seemed not to consider German-Russians as with them in being German.

...

German-Russians could easily be identified in any American community as having come from South Russia. Their clothing, foods, architecture, and agricultural practices all revealed varying degrees of Russian influence. Their German dialects were liberally sprinkled with Russian loan words. But, McIntosh County German-Russians here not Russians, even though their Yankee neighbors often referred to them as "Rooshuns" and the United States government sometimes mistakenly listed them in the census as Russians. Only an insignificant number of the Black Sea Germans who settled in North Dakota could converse easily in Russian and they were typically those who had served in the Russian army or those who had attended school for more than the average number of years in Russia. During a century in South Russia, German-Russians had not mingled with the Russians and they had only rarely intermarried with them. " '... My father was never a Russian,' "boasted one Volga German-Russian, and " ' no Russian blood curses my veins, even though I came into the world in Russia.' "

...

Proud of the fact that they had lived in South Russia for many generations and had yet remained isolated from the Russians; gratified that their blood had not been mingled with that of Russians through intermarriage; stung by being referred to as "Rooshuns" by their insensitive Yankee neighbors; and relieved that, unlike those who had remained in South Russia, they had been spared the ravages of war, revolution, forced migration, and starvation - McIntosh County German-Russians clearly did not consider themselves to be Russians.

...

Among the most difficult cultural adjustments that German-Russians had to make was to switch from using German to using English, particularly in their church services. German-Russians would have fought God Himself had He suggested that worship services could be conducted in a language other than German. "Yes," German-Russian parents might reassure their children, "Our Lord God knows everything - but He cannot understand the heathen babbling that is English." As late as World War II, many McIntosh County churches conducted at least some of their worship services and Bible studies in German. Until the 1930s many children did not learn English until they started school. Portions of the Wishek News were printed in German until 1944 and parts of the Ashley Tribune in German until 1955.

Language was only one means by which German-Russians maintained their identity. They came to America with an established set of minority group defenses that was rare among immigrants. Isolated on the Russian steppes, they had perfected the mechanisms of survival amid alien surroundings. Latecomers to Dakota, they settled on the poorer land, farther from the rivers, railroads, and cities. Distance, bad roads, and a deliberate avoidance of using English separated them from people they considered to be "outsiders." Thus isolated, McIntosh County German-Russians could maintain a way of life largely unaffected by outside influences.

...

German-Russians were admirably equipped for living on the prairies of McIntosh County. The land was their life. They were accustomed to hard and tedious work. They were thrifty to an extreme and adamant to the point of being stubborn. They were independent, self-sufficient, and resourceful. They bore and survived adversity. Aleksandr Solzhenitsyn in his Gulag Archipelago wrote of the methodical German-Russians that they were good husbandmen and indefatigable workers. "Is there any wilderness on earth," he asked, "which [German-Russians] could not turn into a land of plenty?" And wherever the German-Russians went, he noted, they settled in, "not temporarily, ... but forever." "Not for nothing," therefore, "did Russians say in the old days that 'a German is like a willow tree - stick it anywhere and it will take!' " And German-Russians "took" in McIntosh County.

Chapter 3 - Huethers in North Dakota

The Paul Huether Family
Carolina, Henry, Christ, John, Maggie, Katie, Rosie
Mother holding Barbara, Father holding Margret

Paul Huether Jr. was born January 31, 1853 in Peterstal, Russia and died September 8, 1918 near Moses Lake, Washington. He is buried in the Rocky Coulee, Ottmar Cemetery near Wheeler, Washington. The local residents refer to this cemetery as the "Old" Keller Cemetery. Paul married twice; he married Katherina Elisabeth Riedlinger on December 27, 1877 in Johannesthal. They had six children.

Katharine Riedlinger was born December 18, 1854 in Grossliebental and died in Campbell County, South Dakota on February 4, 1892. She left him with six motherless children. Paul then married Katherine T. Becker March 12, 1892 in Campbell County, South Dakota. She was born September 23, 1868 in Kassel and died September 18, 1948 at Walla Walla, Washington. She is buried in the same Cemetery as Paul Jr. They had 10 children.

Paul immigrated to the United States in March 1889 and homesteaded in Campbell County, South Dakota in 1893. He homesteaded Section 14, Township N, Range 75 W. Paul and his family are on the South Dakota 1900 Federal Census and living in Campbell County, South Dakota.

Descendants of Ludwig HUETHER - Third Generation

Family Tree Third Generation

Paul HUETHER Jr. (1853-1918)
+Katherina Elisabeth REIDLINGER (1854 – 1892)
Johannes R. HUETHER (1879 – 1924)
Magdalena HUETHER (1881 – 1932)
Katherina HUETHER (1883 – 1977)
Christian R. HUETHER (1885 – 1977)
Rosina HUETHER (1887 – 1976)
Heinrich HUETHER (1889 – 1964)
+Katherine BECKER (1868 – 1948)
Karolina HUETHER (1892 – 1953)
Margaretha HUETHER (1894 – 1916)
Barbara HUETHER (1895 – 1994)
Andreas HUETHER (1896 – 1970)
Lydia HUETHER (1899 – 2001)
Paul Eugene HUETHER III (1900 – 1950)
Sophia HUETHER (1902 – 1970)
Eva HUETHER (1904 – 1989)
Arlene HUETHER (1906 – 2003)
Jacob HUETHER (1908 – 1966)

15. **Paul HUETHER Jr.** (Paul , Ludwig Jacob) was born 19 Jan 1853 in Peterstal, South Russia. He died 8 Sep 1918 in near Moses Lake, Washington and was buried in country cemetery near Moses Lake Washington.
He immigrated to the US in March 1889. He homesteaded in Campbell County South Dakota in 1893 and then moved to Washington State in 1908. The 1920 Grant County Washington census spells this family's name Herether. Paul and his wife second wife Katherine are both buried at the Rocky Coulee (Ottmar) Cemetery near Wheeler, Washington. It was reported that Paul died of pyaemia (blood poisoning) resulting from an abrasion on a finger.

Paul also married (1) **Katharina Elisabeth REIDLINGER**, daughter of Wilhelm REIDLINGER and Katharina HELFENSTEIN, on 27 Dec 1877 in Johannesthal, S. Russia. Katharina was born 18 Dec 1854 in Grossliebental, S. Russia. She died 10 Jan 1892 in Sutley, South Dakota.
They had the following children:

39 M xi **Johannes R. HUETHER** "John" was born 13 Sep 1879 in Akerman, S. Russia. He died 25 Sep 1924 in Ruff, WA.

40 F xii **Magdalena HUETHER** was born 17 Feb 1881 in Paulsthal, S. Russia. She died after 1932 in Spokane, WA.

41 F xiii **Katherina HUETHER** was born 24 Jan 1883 in Neusatz, S. Russia. She died 27 Dec 1977 in Ashley, SD.

42 M xiv **Christian R. HUETHER** was born 17 Mar 1885 in Neusatz, S. Russia. He died 15 Nov 1966 in Walla Walla, WA.

43 F xv **Rosina HUETHER** "Rose" was born 28 Jan 1887 in Kareson, S. Russia. She died 3 Feb 1976 in Walla Walla, WA.

44 M xvi **Heinrich HUETHER** "Henry" was born 13 Jul 1889 in Campbell Co., SD. He died 1964 in Walla Walla, WA.

Paul married (2) **Katherine T. BECKER** on 12 Mar 1892 in Campbell County, South Dakota. Katherine was born 23 Sep 1868 in Kassel, Russia. She died 18 Sep 1948 in Walla Walla, Washington.

They had the following children:

	29	F	i	**Karolina Bertha HUETHER** "Carolina" was born 3 Dec 1892 in Sutley, SD. She died 25 Mar 1953 in Lewiston, ID.
	30	F	ii	**Margaretha HUETHER** was born 7 Apr 1894 in Sutley, SD. She died 1916.
+	31	F	iii	**Barbara HUETHER** was born 23 Aug 1895 and died 3 Jul 1994.
	32	M	iv	**Andreas HUETHER** "Andrew" was born 21 Nov 1896 in Campbell Co., SD. He died before 1970.
	33	F	v	**Lydia HUETHER** was born 16 Mar 1899 in Campbell Co. SD. She died 21 Apr 2001 in WA.
	34	M	vi	**Paul Eugene Immanuel HUETHER III** was born 27 Oct 1900 in Eureka, SD. He died 29 May 1950 in Chewelah, WA.
	35	F	vii	**Sophia HUETHER** "Sofia" was born 1902 in SD. She died before 1970.
	36	F	viii	**Eva E. HUETHER** was born 13 Sep 1904 in SD. She died 27 May 1989 in Opportunity, WA.
	37	F	ix	**Arlene A. HUETHER** "Adeline" was born 8 Jul 1906 in WA. She died 15 Feb 2003 in San Diego, CA.
	38	M	x	**Jacob S. HUETHER** "Jack" was born 24 Dec 1908 in WA. He died 8 Apr 1966 in San Joaquin Co. CA.

Chapter 4 – Huethers in Washington

"Mother age about 81",
Barbara's Nagel's mother Katherine Huether,
Taken at Gertie's, about 1945;
She died in 1948 or 49 at age 81 or 83;
Barbara said she married a younger man and took some years off.

Aunt Maggie (Barbara's Sister – Stienbach) (?could be aunt Lydia?), Katherine Huether (grandma to Edna), Eva Hoefner (Barbara's sister) Barbara Nagel (grandma)

In 1908 Paul and his family moved by wagon to Washington state, near Moses Lake and settled near relatives Johann Gottlob Hochstatter and his wife Maria Barbara Huether. Paul's father Paul Sr. had moved to the area three years before in 1905.

Rocky Coulee

Paul Huether Sr. had land near Rocky Coulee. Rocky Coulee runs east and west just north of I90 on the east side of Moses Lake. A coulee (or coulée from the French) refers to a kind of valley or drainage zone; the dry, braided channels formed by glacial drainage of the scablands of eastern Washington.

Paul Huether Sr.'s Land

Deed Record F page 586 shows deed 28842 between Wallace L. Ropp to Paul Huether dated October 1st, 1908 for Southwest quarter of Section 20 in Township 19 North of range 30 in Douglas (later Grant) County containing 160 acres for the sum of $2,880 and to continue a mortgage of $1,100 to Griswald, Hallet & Persons.[3]

This is land east of Wheeler and southwest of Ruff near Rocky Coulee.
The current owners are Brend and Carla Frieshe, 2441 NE RD S, (509) 765-4584. Current tax parcels: 181243000, 181243001, 181242000 and 181242001. Tax parcel 181241000 (East half of quarter) is owned by Jerome W. and Carolyn Keating Trs.

Directions: From I90 take U Road NE north
T19R30S20 is between roads 2 RD NE and 3 RD NE and
S NE and T NE, SW quarter would be at roads 2 NE Road and S NE Road

[3] Grant County Warranty Deed Book Vol. F, page 586

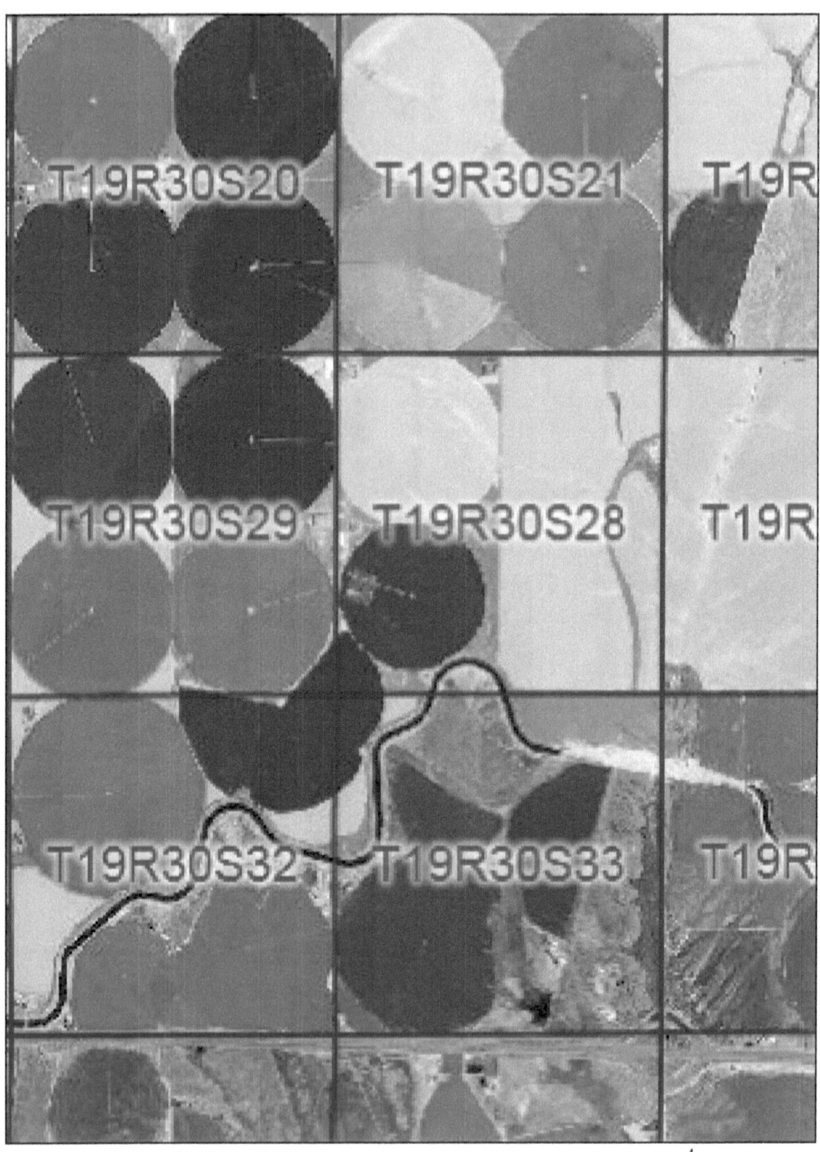

This land is east of Wheeler and south of Ruff near Rocky Coulee.[4]
T19R30S20

[4] http://grantwa.mapsifter.com/default.aspx

Exit 188 from I90 traveling east is Warden and U Rd NE/SE. Just south of this in the picture is Christ Huether's homestead. North several miles and west is Paul Huether Sr.'s property and further north and to the east is the town of Ruff. Picture taken by author July, 2012.

Paul Huether Sr.'s land purchased in 1908. Intersection of Road 2 NE and Road S NE looking northeast. Southwest quarter of Section 20 in Township 19 North of range 30 in Douglas (later Grant) County containing 160 acres (T19R30S20). You can see house and barns in the distance. Picture taken by author July, 2012.

Paul Huether Sr.'s property looking west along the entrance road.
Picture taken by author July, 2012.

The "Pioneer Tree" on the Paul Huether Sr.'s property. The locals called the old trees "Pioneer Trees' because of the age and type of tree that was generally planted by the early pioneers near the homesteads. This tree is over 100 years old and likely planted about 1908 by Paul Huether Sr. Picture taken by author July, 2012.

Paul Huether Sr.'s property looking east. You can see the remnants of the indoor pool with the large barns in the background. Picture taken by author July, 2012.

Paul Huether Sr.'s property looking south across the property from the Pioneer Tree. You can see the remnants of the indoor pool and foundation of the house. Picture taken by author July, 2012.

The original house and out buildings no longer exist but you can place the original house somewhere close to the pioneer tree. To the south of the tree is the foundation of a later house that had an indoor pool. This house burned down. The owner of the house with the indoor pool was caught up in scandal having to do with Ponzi schemes. The current owners have their house across S St. NE from this property.

586 DEED RECORD—F

first part has hereunto set her hand and seal the day and year first above written. ORA MYERS (SEAL) Signed, sealed and delivered in presence of J. M. Pierce, Anna Pierce. THE STATE OF WASHINGTON COUNTY OF DOUGLAS SS.

I, J. M. Pierce, a Notary Public in and for the State of Washington, do hereby certify that on this 28th day of May A.D. 1908, personally appeared before me, Ora Meyers to me known to be the individual described in and who executed the within instrument, and acknowledged that she signed and sealed the same as her free and voluntary act and deed, for the uses and purposes therein mentioned. Given under my hand and official seal, this 28th day of May A.D. 1908. J. M. PIERCE NOTARY PUBLIC, RESIDING AT EPHRATA WASHINGTON. Notary Seal of James M. Pierce. Commission expires Aug. 28, 1908, 190 . Recorded 10/20/08 ,190 . Filed for record on the 19 day of Oct. A.D. 1908, at 1 o'clock and...minutes, P.M., at the request of Mary McGrath. Chas. F. Will, County Auditor. Olive M. Coleman, Deputy. Recorded in Book "33" of Deed, Page 521, Records of Douglas County.

28842. Deed Wallace L. Ropp to Paul Huether.

This Indenture, Made this First day of October A.D. 1908, between Wallace L. Ropp, a bachelor of the County of Stanislaus, State of California party of the first part, and Paul Huether of the County of Douglas, State of Washington party of the second part, Witnesseth: That the said party of the first part, for and in consideration of the sum of Two Thousand Eight Hundred Eighty ($2880.00) 00/100 Dollars, to him in hand paid by the said party of the second part, the receipt whereof is hereby acknowledged, does thereby grant, bargain, sell and convey, unto the said party of the second part, his heirs, and assigns forever, all that tract or parcel of land lying and being in the county of Douglas, and State of Washington and described as follows, to-wit: The Southwest quarter (SW¼) of Section Twenty (20) in Township Nineteen (19) North of range Thirty (30) E.W.M. containing One Hundred Sixty (160) acres more or less according to the Government survey. TO HAVE AND TO HOLD THE SAME, Together with all the hereditaments and appurtenances thereunto belonging, or in anywise appertaining, to the said party of the second part, his heirs and assigns forever. And the said Wallace L. Ropp party of the first part, for himself and for his heirs, executors and administrators, does covenant with the said party of the second part his heirs and assigns, that he is well seized in fee of the lands and premises aforesaid, and has good right to sell and convey the same in manner and form aforesaid; that the same are free from all encumbrances, except one certain First mortgage of Eleven Hundred ($1100.00) Dollars given to Griswald, Hallett & Persons, which mortgage second party assumes and agrees to pay. And the above bargained and granted lands and premises, in the quiet and peaceable possession of said party of the second part, his heirs and assigns, against all persons lawfully claiming, or to claim, the whole or any part thereof, the said part of the first part will warrant and defend. In Testimony Whereof The said party of the first part has hereunto set his hand and seal the day and year first above written. WALLACE L. ROPP (SEAL) Signed, Sealed and Delivered in Presence of A.B. Buford, A. Child. THE STATE OF CALIFORNIA COUNTY OF STANISLAUS SS.

I, B. W. Child, a Notary Public in and for the State of Washington, do hereby certify that on this 12th day of October A.D. 1908, personally appeared before me Wallace L. Ropp to me known to be the individual described in and who executed the within instrument, and acknowledged that he signed and sealed the same as his free and voluntary act and deed, for the uses and purposes therein mentioned. Given under my hand and official seal, this 12th day of October A.D. 1908. B. W. CHILD NOTARY PUBLIC. RESIDING AT TARLOCK, CALIF. NOTARY PUBLIC IN AND FOR THE COUNTY OF STANISLAUS, STATE OF CALIFORNIA. Notary Seal of B.W. Child. Commission expires My commission expires Oct. 17, 1912. Recorded 10/22/08 ,190 . Filed for record the 20 day of Oct A.D. 1908, at 1 o'clock and...minutes P.M., at the request of Farmers Bank Krupp. Chas. F. Will, County Auditor, Olive M. Coleman, Deputy. Recorded in Book "33" Deeds, Page 523, Records of Douglas County.

28847 Deed M. H. Sorell et ux to L. W. Stetson

This Indenture, Made this 22nd day of September A.D. 1908, between M. H. Sorell and Emma Sorell, his wife parties of the first part, and L. W. Stetson party of the second part, Witnesseth, That the said parties of the first part, for and in consideration of the sum of

Grant County Deed Book F, Page 586 Warranty Deed to Paul Huether, 1908

In the 1910 Grant County U.S. Census Paul Huether Jr. age 58 and Katherina age 41 both born in Russia are listed as living in Wheeler.[5] Living with Paul and Katherina are son Henry age 20, daughters Caroline age 17, Margrette age 16, Barbara age 14, son Andrew age 13, daughter Lydia age 11, son Paul Jr. age 10, daughter Sophia age 8, daughters E. E. (Eva) age 6, and Adeline age 4 and son Jacob S. age 1 and 3 months.

		———	H. F.	Son	M	W	12	S	Nebraska	Pennsylvania	Pennsylvania	English	Farm labour	Home farm
		———	E. A.	Son	M	W	5	S	Washington	Pennsylvania	Pennsylvania		None	
87	87	Huether	Paul	Head	M	W	58	M2	Russ German	Russ German	Russ German	German	Farmer	General farm
		———	Katherina	Wife	F	W	41	M	Russ German	Russ German	Russ German	German	None	
		———	Henry	Son	M	W	20	S	South Dakota	Russ German	Russ German	English	Farm labour	Home farm

Huether	Caroline	Daughter	F	W	17	S	South Dakota	Russ German	Russ German
———	Margrette	Daughter	F	W	16	S	South Dakota	Russ German	Russ German
———	Barbara	Daughter	F	W	14	S	South Dakota	Russ German	Russ German
———	Andrew	Son	M	W	13	S	South Dakota	Russ German	Russ German
———	Lydia	Daughter	F	W	11	S	South Dakota	Russ German	Russ German
———	Paul Jr	Son	M	W	10	S	South Dakota	Russ German	Russ German
———	Sophia	Daughter	F	W	8	S	South Dakota	Russ German	Russ German
———	E. E.	Daughter	F	W	6	S	South Dakota	Russ German	Russ German
———	Adelina	Daughter	F	W	4	S	Washington	Russ German	Russ German
———	Jacob S.	Son	M	W	1 3/12	S	Washington	Russ German	Russ German

Also in the 1910 Grant County U.S. Census Gottlieb Hochstatter age 57 with wife Barbara age 55 both born in Russia are listed living in Moses Lake with son John 30, daughters Sophia 28 and Katie age 19, and son Gottlieb age 11. The Ottmars are also listed in Grant County. William age 53, Maggie age 49, John age 43, Caroline age 41, Jacob age 36, Barbara age 34, John Jr. age 14, Jacob Jr. age 13, John and Lizzie age 11, and Barbara and ward age 9.[6]

The 1920 Federal Census for Grant County, Washington lists the family name as Hertether.

---

[5] 1910 U.S. CENSUS, Grant County, Washington; Page 270A, image file 0160.tif, Record ID HRP1910GRT5375

[6] 1910 U.S. CENSUS, Grant County, Washington; Copyright 2001,Eugene Jenkins, 1381 Longmire Lane, Selah, WA 98942http://www.webbitt.com/volga/WA-1910-rus.txt

Christ Huether's Homestead

Christ Huether homesteaded for land lots 1 & 2 quarter of section No. 4 in Township No 18N Range No. 30 containing 56 acres before Dec. 24, 1907.[7] He secured the Land Patent (certificate No. 3635) for the homestead on the 24th of April, 1920.

At the corner of S. 5 SE and I90 Frontage Road looking southeast. Christ Huether's land was 86 acres - Lots one and two of section four in Township eighteen north of Range thirty (T18R30S4). Maps of the lots have not been found but counting from top to bottom and left to right would place the lots at the northwest corner. 86 acres is about ½ of a quarter section. Picture taken by author July, 2012.

[7]Christ Huether Homestead, Grant County Final Receipt Vol. B pages 105-106

Christ R. Huether's homestead, 1920. The land was Lots one and two of section four in Township eighteen north of Range thirty (T18R30S04) containing 86 This land is Southwest of the I90 and U RD Interchange[8]

[8] http://grantwa.mapsifter.com/default.aspx

No. 3635 25099. Receivers Office at Waterville, Wash. Dec. 24 1907. Received from Christ R. Huether of Douglas County Washington, the sum of two hundred & sixteen dollars

30 cents; being in full for the lots 1 & 2 quarter of section No. 4 in township No. 18N range No. 30 E W M containing 56 acres, and 52 hundredths, at $-- per acre. $216.30 W. A. HENRY RECEIVER. $1.30 testimony fee received. number of written words 623 --rate per 100 words 22½ cents. Filed and recorded at the request of I W Matthews on the 11 day of January 1908 at -- minutes past 2 o'clock P. M. Chas. F. Will Auditor. Olive M Coleman Deputy. recorded in book "30" of Deeds page 174 Douglas County records.

###

Christ Huether Homestead, Grant County Final Receipt Vol. B pages 105-106

Christ Huether received his final receipt on a homestead Dec. 24, 1907 for land lots 1 & 2 quarter of section No. 4 in Township No 18N Range No. 30 containing 56 acres.[9]

Christ R. Huether secured a Land Patent (certificate No. 3635) for a homestead on the 24th of April, 1920 registered in Waterville. The land was Lots one and two of section four in Township eighteen north of Range thirty east of Willamette Meridian containing 86 and 52/100s acres (Section 4, Township 18 N, Range 30).

[9] Christ Huether Homestead, Grant County Final Receipt Vol. B pages 105-106

FILE NO. 09610.

THE UNITED STATES OF AMERICA

TO ALL TO WHOM THESE PRESENTS SHALL COME, GREETING:

Certificate No. 3638.

WHEREAS, Christ H. Huether has deposited in the General Land Office of the United States a Certificate of the Register of the Land Office at Waterville, Washington, whereby it appears that full payment has been made by the said Christ H. Huether according to the provisions of the Act of Congress, of the 24th day of April, 1820, entitled "An Act making further provision for the Sale of the Public Lands," and the Acts supplemental thereto for the Lots one and two of Section four in Township eighteen north of Range thirty east of the Willamette Meridian, Washington, containing eighty six and fifty-two hundredths acres,

according to the Official Plat of the survey of the said lands, returned to the General Land Office by the Surveyor General, which said tract has been purchased by the said Christ H. Huether

NOW, KNOW YE, That the United States of America, in consideration of the premises and in conformity with the several acts of Congress in such case made and provided, have given and granted and by these presents do give and grant unto the said Christ H. Huether and to his heirs, the said tract above described, to have and to hold the same, together with all the rights, privileges, immunities and appurtenances of whatsoever nature thereunto belonging unto the said Christ H. Huether and to his heirs and assigns forever, subject to any vested and accrued water rights, for mining, agricultural, manufacturing or other purposes, and rights to ditches and reservoirs used in connection with such water rights as may be recognized and acknowledged by the local customs, laws and decisions of courts, and also subject to the right of the proprietor of a vein or lode to extract and remove his ore therefrom should the same be found to penetrate or intersect the premises hereby granted as provided by law; and there is reserved from the lands hereby granted a right of way thereon for ditches or canals constructed by the authority of the United States.

IN TESTIMONY WHEREOF, I, Theodore Roosevelt President of the United States of America, have caused these letters to be made patent and the Seal of the General Land Office to be hereunto affixed.

Given under my hand at the City of Washington the ninth day of July in the year of our Lord one thousand nine hundred and eight and of the Independence of the United States the one hundred and thirty-third

By the President Theodore Roosevelt

By M. W. Young Secretary.

H. W. Sanford Recorder of the General Land Office.

Recorded 8216 Vol. *** Page ***

Filed and recorded at the request of Connecticut Investment Co. on the 30 day of March, 1917, at *** minutes past 9 o'clock, A. M.

C. T. Sanders, County Auditor.

Deputy.

Grant County Patents Vol. 1, p 459

Quincy

In 1910 Paul Jr. (Barbara's father) bought 80 acres just to the east of Quincy. He sold the land in 1913 for stock in the King County Trading Company. Paul Jr.'s son John R. Huether had purchased 3 lots in the town of Quincy (sometime before 1907). Paul was one of the founding members of the German Reformed Church in 1908. John was an owner of the Idle Hour Bar. In 1909 a sheriff's sale was held and John Huether bought the City Bakery and lunch counter. John R. Huether sold the lots in 1912. Paul Jr. died in 1918. His son John died in Ruff in 1925.

DEED RECORD, No. 3

In Witness Whereof, The said parties of the first part have hereunto set their hands and seals the day and year first above written.
Signed and Sealed in the presence of

William Eadie (Seal)
M.H.Eadie (Seal)

State of Washington,)
: ss.
County of Pierce.)

I, G.S.Perryman a Notary Public in and for the State of Washington, residing at Tacoma in said County, do hereby certify that on this 14th day of April A.D.1910 personally appeared before me William Eadie and M.H.Eadie, husband and wife, to me known to be the individuals described in and who executed the within Instrument and acknowledged that they signed and sealed the same as their free and voluntary act and deed for the uses and purposes therein mentioned.

Given under my hand and official seal, this fourteenth day of April A.D.1910.
G.S.Perryman
Notary Public in and for said State Residing at Tacoma in said County,
Commission expires February 16th 1914.

Notary seal G.S. Perryman.
Commission expires Feb.16,1914.
Filed for record at the request of R.C.Horn...
Dec.2.A.D.1910 at 2.40 P.M.

J.H.Hill, County Auditor.
By *Lettie Shultz* Deputy.

FILE NO. 5588.
WARRANTY DEED.

The Grantor Ben E. Hervey and May Hervey his wife, for and in consideration of Nine hundred and eighty DOLLARS, in hand paid, CONVEY and WARRANT to Paul Huether of Quincy Wash by occupation, residing at the following described real property, situate in the Grant County of State of Washington, to-wit:

South Half of the South East Quarter of Section Eleven Township Twenty North of Range Twenty four W.M. Containing Eighty acres More or less as per the Government Survey together with all the hereditaments and appurtenances thereunto belonging, or in anywise appertaining.
SUBJECT TO
Dated this 15 day of Nov A.D.1910.

Ben E.Hervey
May Hervey

THE STATE OF WASHINGTON.)
: ss.
County of Spokane.)

I, Pauline M.Borgman a Notary Public in and for the State of Washington, do hereby certify that on this 15th day of November A.D.1910, personally appeared before me Ben E.Hervey and May Hervey his wife, to me known to be the indiwidual described in and who executed the within instrument, and acknowledged that they signed and sealed the same as their free and voluntary act and deed, for the uses and purposew therein mentioned.

Given under my hand and official seal, this 15th day of November A.D.1910.
Pauline M. Borgman
Notary Public
Residing at Spokane Washington.

Notary seal Pauline M.Borgman.
Commission expires May 15,1914.
Filed for record at the request of First National Bank Quincy.
December 2.A.D.1910 at 8.40 A.M.

J.H.Hill, County Auditor.
By *Lettie Shultz* Deputy.

FILE NO. 5597.
DEED.

THIS INDENTURE, made this first day of June, A.D.1910, between the Warden Investment Company, a corporation organized and existing under and by virtue of the laws of the State of Washington, and having its principal place of business at *the city of* Spokane, Washington, party of the first part, and P. H.Sherman, of Spokane, Washington, party of the second part, WITNESSETH:

That the said party of the first part, for and in co nsideration of the sum of Five Dollars ($5.00) to it in hand paid by the said party of the second part, the receipt whereof is hereby acknowledged, and other good and valuable considerations, does hereby grant, bargain, sell and convey unto the said party of the second part, his heirs and assigns forever, all the tracts or parcels of land lying and being in the C...

Grant County Deed Book Vol. 3, Page 512, Warranty Deed to Paul Huether, 1910

Deed Record, No. 3 File No. 5588 Warranty Deed lists grantor Ben E. Hervey and his wife May Hervey in consideration of $980 conveys to Paul Huether of Quincy Washington the South Half of the South East Quarter of Section 11, Township 20 north of range 24 containing 80 acres on November 15, 1910.[10]

This land is east of Quincy.

Paul Huether's land bought in 1910 near Quincy Washington. The South Half of the South East Quarter of Section 11, Township 20 north of range 24 containing 80 acres (T20R24S11).[11]

[10] Grant County Warranty Deed Book Vol. 3, page 512

[11] http://grantwa.mapsifter.com/default.aspx

T20R24S11 is off of I90 north on SR281, right turn (east on SR 28 between O RD and Adams RD NW. Current owners are Brad and Phyllis Beirlink.

Directions: head east from Quincy on SR 28 toward Ephrata. Turn left (north) on Adams Road NW. The land is located along SR 28 and Adams Road NW.

STATE OF WASHINGTON }
COUNTY OF GRANT } SS

I, W.G.Matthews a notary public in and for the State of Washington duly commissioned and sworn, do hereby certify that on this 20th day of December A D 1913 personally appeared before me Walter J Hauser husband of Emma Hauser to me personally known to be the individual described in and who executed the within instrument and acknowledged that he signed and sealed the same as his free and voluntary act and deed for the uses and pu purposes therein mentioned; and the said Walter J Hauser being by me first duly sworn did upon his oath say that this deed is not given for the purpose of hindering defrauding or wronging any creditor or creditors whomsoever.

Given under my hand and official seal this 20th day of December A D 1913.

Notary Seal W G Matthews — W G Matthews

Commission expires Mar 5 1917 — Notary Public in and for the above named County and State residing at Ephrata.

Filed for record at request of W J Hauser — J L Pearce County Auditor

Dec 20 A D 1913 at 4 o'clock and 50 minutes P M — By Olive M. Coleman Deputy

FILE NO. 19056

WARRANTY DEED.

THE GRANTOR Paul Huether and Katharina Huether his wife for and in consideration of One Dollar and other considerations of stock of King Co Trading Co Dollars in hand paid convey and warrant to King Co Trading Co the following described real estate:

North half (½) of SE quarter (¼) and SE quarter (¼) of the SE quarter (¼) of section eleven (11) Tp twenty (20) range twenty four (24) E W M. Situated in the County of Grant State of Washington.

Dated this 1st day of November 1913

Witnesses: — Paul Huether (Seal)

(Foreign) Katharina Huether (Seal)

STATE OF WASHINGTON }
COUNTY OF GRANT } SS

I, W M Jenkins a notary public do hereby certify that on this1st day of November 1913 personally appeared before me Paul Huether and Kathara Huether to me known to be the individuals described in and who executed the within instrument and acknowledged that they signed and sealed the same as their free and voluntary act and deed for the uses and purposes therein mentioned.

Given under my hand and official seal this 1st day of November A D 1913.

Notary Seal W M Jenkins — W M Jenkins

Commission expires Aug 10 1915 — Notary Public in and for the State of Washington residing at Wheeler

Filed for record at request of King County Trading Co — J L Pearce County Auditor

Dec 22 1913 at 20 minutes past 8 A M — By Olive M. Coleman Deputy

FILE NO. 19057

WARRANTY DEED.

THE GRANTOR John R Huether for and in consideration of One Dollar and other considerations of Stock of King Co Trading Co Dollars in hand paid convey and warrant to King Co Trading Co the following described real estate:

The west half (½) of Lot three (3) in block four (4) Cochrans Plat of Main Quincy according to the Recorded plat thereof situated in the County of Grant State of

Deed Book 14, Page 211, Warranty Deed Paul Huether Jr. Sells 1913

212

DEED RECORD No. 14

Washington.

Dated this ..... day of .... 19..

Witnesses: John R Huether (Seal)

STATE OF WASHINGTON }
COUNTY OF KING } SS

I W W Sylvester a notary public do hereby certify that on this 18th day of December 1913 personally appeared before me John R Huether to me known to be the individual described in and who executed the within instrument and acknowledged that he signed and sealed the same as his free and voluntary act and deed for the uses and purposes therein mentioned.

Given under my hand and official seal this 18th day of December A D 1913

W W Sylvester Notary Seal W W Sylvester

Commission expires Nov 16 1917 Notary Public in and for the State of Washington residing at Issaquah

Filed for record at request of King Co Trading Co J L Pearce County Auditor

Dec 22 1913 at 25 minutes past 8 A M By [signature] Deputy

Grant County Deed Book Vol. 14, Page 212

Paul Huether and Katherina Huether sold the North half of SE quarter and SE quarter of South East quarter of section 11, township 20 Range 24 in Grant County to King Co. Trading Co. for one dollar and stock. November 1st, 1913.[12] This is a sale of part of the previous deed above.

12 Grant County Deed Book Vol. 14, Page 211

26130 Quit Claim Deed. Statutory From. The Grantor John R. Huether an unmarried man of Quincy, in the county of Douglas and state of Washington, for the consideration of one (1) Dollars, in hand paid conveys and quit claims to John Zeller of Quincy, in the county of Douglas in the state of Washington all interest in the following described real estate lot four (4) in block six (6) in Original Town of Quincy, Washington, according to the recorded plat thereof situated in the county of Douglas, state of Washington. Dated this twentieth (20) day of August 1908. JOHN R. HUETHER (SEAL).

State of Washington County of Douglas ss I, Axel E. Jonson a Notary Public do hereby certify that on this twentieth (20) day of August 1908 personally appeared before me John R. Huether and unmarried man to me known to be the individual described in and who executed the within instrument, and acknowledged that he signed and sealed the same as his free and voluntary act and deed, for the uses and purposes therein mentioned. Given under my hand and official seal this ninteenth (19) day of August A D 1908. AXEL E. JONSON Notary Public in and for the state of Washington residing at Quincy. Notary Seal Axel E.Jonson Commission expires Sep. 8, 1911. Filed for record at request of The First Nat'l Bank of Quincy Aug. 26 A D 1908 at 1. 00 P:M. Recorded 8-26-08. Chas. F. Will County Auditor. By Bertha L. Rock Deputy. recorded in book "35" of Deeds page 565 Douglas County records.

John R. Huether Grant County Quick Claim Deed (QED) Vol. 14, pages 8-9

John R. Huether, unmarried man of Quincy Washington, quit claims to John Zeller of Quincy on August 19th, 1908 for land lot 4 in block 6 in Original Town of Quincy Washington according to plat thereof situated in the county of Douglas and recorded in book "35" of Deeds page 565 Douglas County records.[13]

Lot 4 is present day address 214 B St. SE in Quincy.

In 1913 John R. Huether also sells to King County Trading Co. west half of lot 3 in block 4 Cochrane Plat of Quincy in Grant County. John R. Huether is Paul Jr.'s eldest son and Barbara's brother.[14]

Lot 3 is present day 216 B St. SE in Quincy. This is the site of Idle Hour Saloon that John owned and was later moved two blocks west; more on that later.

---

[13] John R. Huether Grant County Quick Claim Deed (QED) Vol. 14, pages 8-9

[14] Grant County Deed Book Vol. 14, Page 211

210 SE B St, Quincy, Washington. John R Huether owned lots 3,4 and 5 which correspond to 210(lot 5), 214(lot 4 and lot 3) SE B. St.[15]

[15] http://grantwa.mapsifter.com/default.aspx

FILE NO 15143
WARRANTY DEED

THE GRANTOR John R. Huether of Quincy, Grant County, State of Washington, a elor for and in consideration of one dollar and other valuable consideration in hand , conveys and warrants to John L. Field, the grantee the following described real es-. Lot five (5) in Block Six (6) of the original town of Quincy, Grant County, State ashington, according to the recorded plat thereof. Situated in the County of Grant, e of Washington.

Dated July 3rd A. D. 1912.
ned in presence of John R. Huether, SEAL
. Lovejoy

E OF WASHINGTON)
} ss
TY OF KING }

THIS IS TO CERTIFY that on this 3d day of July A. D. 1912 before me M. W. ejoy, a Notary Public in and for the State of Washington duly commissioned and sworn onally came John R. Huether, a bachelor, to me known to be the individual described and who executed the within instrument and acknowledged to me that he signed and led the same as his free and voluntary act and deed for the uses and purposes therein tioned.

Witness my hand and official seal the day and year in this certificate first ve written.
ary Seal, M. W. Lovejoy
mission expires April 25 1914.

M. W. Lovejoy, Notary Public in and for the State of Washington residing at Seattle.

ed for record at the request of R. B. Woten
day of Jan 1913 at 25 mins past 8 A. M. J. L. Pearce, County Auditor.
By J.W. Ramsay
Deputy

Grant County Warranty Deed Book Vol. 12, page 529

Seller John R. Huether of Quincy conveyed to John L. Field Lot 5 in Block 6 or original town of Quincy according to recorded plat on July 3rd, 1912.[16] Lot 5 is 210 B St. SE in Quincy.

[16] Grant County Warranty Deed Book Vol. 12, page 529

German Reformed Lutheran Church

The first church in Quincy was the Congregational Church opened in 1904. From the historical description: "Built in 1904, this was the first church in Quincy, serving the entire Protestant, German-Russian community. As other churches were organized and built, this because the German Lutheran Church, 1907-1953. The second church was the Presbyterian Church begun in 1905 and was English speaking. Both of these churches are still in Quincy.

In 1908 Paul Huether was a founding member of the German speaking German Reformed Church. Paul Sr. was one of the people instrumental in organizing the Odessa Reformed Church in Sutley, Campbell County, South Dakota. Faye Morris in *They Claimed the Desert* described the church:[17]

> The third Church in the town of Quincy was the German Reformed Church. About a year after the congregation was organized they were able to build, planned to cost $1,200, the building was dedicated in October of 1909. Rev. Peter Schild who had just graduated from a seminary in Wisconsin, was the pastor of this German speaking church and he remained until 1921. The thirteen charter members were John Baur, Philipp and Jacob Dormaier, Paul Heuther [SIC], Balzar Hieb, Wilhelm Ottman, Frederick Rennick, Philipp Schatz, Chirstain, Jacob and William Shirzman, Michael Serr, and George Stoller. In 1954 a new church was build and combined with the Congregational Christrian members to be known as the United Church of Christ of Today. The old building was finally torn down and replaced by the Security Bank [now the Washington Trust Bank].

The thirteen charter members of the German Reformed Church:

Philip and Jacob Dormaier

Christ Dormaier married into the Hochstatter family and moved to Ruff to run a garage. Martin Dormaier is likely involved with John Nagel in financial transactions in the late 1920s. Philipp Dormaier with his wife and fourteen children moved from South Dakota. Johnny Dormaier ran a general store destroyed by fire in 1917.

Christian, Jacob and William Schorzman

Migrated from Russia to South Dakota and arrived in Quincy in 1902. Several son in laws were also founding members fo the church. Bill Schozman

---

[17] Morris, Faye, *They Claimed the Desert*, Ye Galleon Press, Fairfield, Washington, 1976, p. 248

married Rebecca Reimann. The Reiman brothers where from the Dakotas and then farmed in Odessa before moving to Quincy.

Balzar Hieb
Son in law to Schorzman family. Married Katherine Schorzman. He had a large brick house in town and grew apples and grapes.

Philipp Schatz
Son in law to Schorzman family. Married Christina Schorzman. Came to Quincy in 1902 and was the first to open a general store in partnership with Balzar Hieb his brother in-law. Their brother in law bought out the business in 1910. Adam Schatz later married Margaret Huether.

John Bauer
Son in law to Schorzman family. Married Sophie Schorzman.

George Stoller
Had a milk route.

Wilhelm Ottman, Michael Serr, Frederick Rennick
No further information.

The German Reformed Church, 1911 from *They Claimed the Desert* page 250

Site of German Reformed Church is now the Washington Trust Bank on Central Ave.

"Barbara Huether (Nagel) confirmation class graduation from Lutheran Church
About 15 years old, Barbara is tall one on end (1910)
Lutheran Minister in center; Moses Lake, Washington"
From back of picture

(although on the back this is listed as Moses Lake, Moses Lake was Neppel at the time so this was labeled much after the picture was taken. In 1910 Barbara's father Paul Jr. had land near Quincy. This same picture unlabeled except for "Communion, June 11, 1911" is attributed to the German Reformed Church, 1911 in Quincy, Washington by *They Claimed the Desert* page 251

The Idle Hour Saloon

The Idle Hour was just east of Hieb & Schatx store while Burmaster's "Hub" was the next building to the east of the Idle Hour. The Idle Hour was moved one block east in about 1910 and eventually became a pool room and now a tavern. John Heuther [SIC] in apron.[18]

Faye Morris in *They Claimed the Desert* described the ownership of the Idle Hour Saloon first started by Charley and Ed Sapp as the first saloon in Quincy:[19]

> J. H. Burmaster took over the Sapp's saloon in January of 1905 and called it the "Hub". He enjoyed a good business and in March erected a new building to the west of the printing office. In the fall of 1906 John Zeller was the owner and sold a half interest in lots 4 & 5, block 6 of original Quincy to John Heuther [SIC] for $375. They called it the "Idle Hour".

Faye Morris in *They Claimed the Desert* quoted the Quincy Quill, the local newspaper on the Idle Hour:[20]

---

[18] Morris, Faye, *They Claimed the Desert*, Ye Galleon Press, Fairfield, Washington, 1976, p. 120
[19] Morris, Faye, *The Birth of a Town*, appears self-published, p. 18

From the QQ: "The big owl mascot kept by Messrs, Zeller & Heuther [SIC] in the Idle Hour Saloon, took a notion Sunday evening about seven o'clock to take a little vacation. As the closing laws were on, the owl got lonesome or else went out to drum up trade, and not waiting for an open door, it took a header for a top pane of glass, which was about four feet square. Its aim was only too good, and likewise its speed. The sidewalk caught the glass, and the wire netting in front of the tennis court near Moden's store caught the owl. There it sat on the top wire when John Zeller arrived on the scene. The meeting was very affectionate. John reached up his hand the owl reached down his claw. The two met in a long, fond clasp, mostly too long and too fond for Mr. Zeller, who had some difficulty in making Mr. Owl understand that he was not giving him signs of any new secret order. The owl is now back at his old stand in the Idle Hour".

Mr. Zeller quit the business in August of 1908 and the bar closed, as Heuther [SIC] had taken charge of the bar at the Victoria Hotel three months before. C. C. Morton who had worked at the Victoria, opened "The Idle Hour" again in 1912.

[20] Morris, Faye, *They Claimed the Desert*, Ye Galleon Press, Fairfield, Washington, 1976, p. 120

Victoria Hotel

The Victoria Hotel shut for a while until 1920 and then burned down in 1929 to be replaced with a post office building which is now used as a ceramic shop.[21]

John Huether was in charge of the bar at the Victoria Hotel in 1908. The hotel was built in 1906. The German-American State Bank had a temporary place of business in the Victoria Hotel until their brick building was completed. The bank later changed its name in 1908 to The National Bank of Quincy and later to the Quincy Valley State Bank.

[21] Morris, Faye, *The Birth of a Town*, appears self-published, pp. 59,60

Victoria Hotel from a post card[22]

[22] http://www.historylink.org/index.cfm?DisplayPage=output.cfm&file_id=5362

Ruff

On February 27th, 1924 Christ Huether bought from Katharina Huether the contents of a hotel located in the town of Ruff, Grant County including the post office fixtures, safe lock boxes and all of the hotel furnishings, a five passenger car engine for a Model 4 T, a Ford Roadster with a truck body, and one half interest in Keystone well drilling outfit consisting of drill, gas engine and all tools. The deed was filed on behalf of Ruff Hardware & Imp. Co., Ruff, Washington. Christ and Elizabeth Huether sold this to Emilia Huether in March of 1925.

FILE NO. 44637.

BILL OF SALE.

KNOW ALL MEN BY THESE PRESENTS, That We, J. B. Huether & Amelia Huether, his wife the party of the first part, for and in consideration of the sum of One Dollar & Consideration DOLLARS, to me in hand paid by Christ B. Huether the parties of the second part, the receipt whereof is hereby acknowledged, do by these presents grant, bargain, sell, convey and confirm unto the said party of the second part, his executors, administrators and assigns, the following described personal property, located and being in Ruff County of Grant State of Washington to-wit: All post office fixtures, including safe lock boxes and all other articles belonging thereto. All furnishing for hotel, house hold goods and all other articles in or about building. 1-Baby Overland five pass-car-Engine #75524-Model 4 T. 1-Ford Roadster with truck body. One half interest in Keystone well drilling outfit consisting of drill, gas engine and all tools, repairs and such belonging thereto, said drill is now in Yakima County under care of J. J. Wetter who is also one half owner.

TO HAVE AND TO HOLD the same to the said party of the second part, his executors, administrators and assigns, forever.

And J. B. Huether & Amelia Huether do for their heirs, executors and administrators, covenant and agree to and with the said party of the second part, his executors, administrators and assigns, to warrant and defend the sale of such property, goods and chattels hereby made unto the said party of the second part, his executors, and assigns, against all and every person and persons whomsoever, lawfully claiming or to claim the same.

IN TESTIMONY WHEREOF, We have hereunto set our hands and seals the 23rd day of Feb., in the year of our Lord, one thousand nine hundred and Twenty four.

Signed, Sealed and Delivered in Presence of Katharina Huether

J. B. Huether (SEAL)

Amilia
Mrs. ~~J. B.~~ Huether (SEAL)

STATE OF Washington }
County of Grant } ss.

I, Roy Swigart, a Notary Public in and for said County and State, do hereby certify that on this 23 day of Feb. A. D. 1924, personally appeared before me J. B. Huether & Amelia Huether to me known to be the individuals described in and who executed the within instrument, and acknowledged that they signed and sealed the same as their free and voluntary act and deed, for the uses and purposes therein mentioned.

Given under my hand and official seal this 23 day of Feb. A. D. 1924.

NOTARY SEAL: ROY SWIGART, NOTARY PUBLIC, STATE OF WASHINGTON, COMMISSION EXPIRES APR. 7, 1926

Roy Swigart Notary Public in and for the State of Washington Residing at Ruff

Filed for record at request of Ruff Hardware & Imp. Co., Ruff, Wash. on the 27th day of Feb., 1924 at 15 minutes past 1 P. M.

W. W. KINSEY, COUNTY AUDITOR.

BY [signature] DEPUTY.

Adams County Miscellaneous Records, Vol. C, p 221

FILE NO.48650
BILL OF SALE

KNOW ALL MEN BY THESE PRESENTS, That We, C.H.Huether, and Elizabeth Huether, his wife, the parties of the first part, for and in consideration of the sum of one dollar and other considerations DOLLARS, to me in hand paid by Emilia Huether the party of the second part, the receipt whereof is hereby acknowledged, do by these presents grant, bargain, sell, convey and confirm unto the said party of the second part, her executors, administrators and assigns, the following described personal property, located and being in Ruff County of Grant State of Washington to-wit:

all Post Office fixtures including safe, lock boxes and all other articles belonging thereto. All furnishings for hotel, household goods and all other articles in or about building, one Baby Overland five passenger car engine No.76524 Model 47, one Ford roadster with truck body. One half interest in Keystone well drilling outfit consisting of drill, gas engine and all tools, repairs etc. belonging thereto. said drill is now in Yakima County, Wash.

TO HAVE AND TO HOLD the same to the said party of the second part, her executors, administrators and assigns, forever.

And C.H.Huether and Elizabeth Huether do for their heirs, executors and administrators, covenant and agree to and with the said party of the second part, her executors, administrators and assigns, to warrant and defend the sale of such property, goods and chattels hereby made unto the said party of the second part, her executors, and assigns, against all and every person and persons whomsoever, lawfully claiming or to claim the same.

IN TESTIMONY WHEREOF, We have hereunto set our hands and seals the 2nd day of March, in the year of Our Lord, One thousand nine hundred and twenty five

Signed, Sealed and Delivered in presence of W.B.Fullerwider

C H Huether (Seal)
Elizabeth Huether (Seal)

STATE OF WASHINGTON |
| ss.
COUNTY OF GRANT |

I, W.B.Fullerwider, a Notary Public in and for said County and State, do hereby certify that on this 2nd day of March A.D.1925, personally appeared before me C.H.Huether and Elizabeth Huether, his wife, to me known to be the individuals described in and who executed the within instrument, and acknowledged that they signed and sealed the same as their free and voluntary act and deed, for the uses and purposes therein mentioned.

Given under my hand and official seal this 2nd day of March A.D.1925.

NOTARY SEAL W.B.FULLERWIDER NOTARY PUBLIC STATE OF WASHINGTON COMMISSION EXPIRES FEB.2, 1929.

W.B.Fullerwider Notary Public in and for the State of Washington Residing at Ritzville

Filed for Record MAR.4th.1925 at 1:15 P.M., Request of Ruff Hdwe.& Imp.Co., Ruff, Washington.

G.W.LIBBEY, County Auditor
By Valerie French Deputy.

Adams County Miscellaneous Records, Vol. C, p 293

Directions: take road U off of I90 and head north
turn left (east) on Road 3 NE
Turn left (north) on road W NE
Ruff is on the right (east) about 2 miles, there are several roads.
Video of town:
http://www.youtube.com/watch?v=YrEuXyxaV2I

The town of Ruff (pronouced "Roof". The streets have been renamed. They used to be 1st and 2nd street. The Ruff Hotel is located at the SE corner of Main St. (Lewis St. NE on some maps) and 1st Ave NE (Road W 2 NE on some maps). All that is left of the hotel is the foundation. There is a grain elevator in town, one good house on Clark St NE and several barns – the rest now is a few mobile homes. The lady at the good house seems to own most of the town and rents out some of the mobile homes. She raises horses and seems nice. The railroad used to have tracks through here but they were taken up years ago.
http://grantwa.mapsifter.com/default.aspx

Looking northeast across Rocky Coulee to the town of Ruff.
Picture taken by author July, 2012.

Approach to the town of Ruff. Picture taken by author July, 2012.

The one good house on Clark St NE. The lady at the good house seems to own most of the town and rents out some of the mobile homes. She raises horses and seems nice.
Picture taken by author July, 2012.

Looking south down 1st Ave. The Hotel foundation is to the left in the picture.
Picture taken by author July, 2012.

The Hotel foundation is all that is left.
Picture taken by author July, 2012.

Chapter 5 - Paul Huether's Family in Washington

These are **Barbara** Nagel's brothers and sisters. John R. Huether owned land in Quincy. Magdalena was known as Aunt Maggie. Paul Eugene Huether was Barbara's brother. Christ Huether homesteaded in Grant County and then moved to Rathdrum. He likely influenced the Nagels to move to Rathdrum once they lost the land in Lind. Eva lived nearby in Spokane.

Barbara Nagel's mother, Katherine Huether
Taken 12th of September 1948, died in 1949 next spring

Family Tree Third Generation in Washington

Paul HUETHER Jr. (1853-1918)
+Katherina Elisabeth REIDLINGER (1854 – 1892)
    Johannes R. HUETHER (1879 – 1924)
    +Emilie METTLER (1883 – 1973)
        Herbert (1916 – 1983)
        Ruth (1917 -)
        Verna (1920 -)
        Leona (1922 -)
    Magdalena HUETHER (1881 – 1932)
    Katherina HUETHER (1883 – 1977)
    Christian R. HUETHER (1885 – 1977)
    +Elizabeth HOCHSTETTER (1887 – 1949)
        Reinhold (1919 – 1954)
        Leo (1910 – 1952)
        Elizabeth (1916 – 1972)
        Frieda (1918 -)
        Herman (1919 -)
    +Lydia WEIS (1890 – 1983)
    Rosina HUETHER (1887 – 1976)
    Heinrich HUETHER (1889 – 1964)
+Katherine BECKER (1868 – 1948)
    Karolina HUETHER (1892 – 1953)
    Margaretha HUETHER (1894 – 1916)
    Barbara HUETHER (1895 – 1994)
    Andreas HUETHER (1896 – 1970)
    Lydia HUETHER (1899 – 2001)
    Paul Eugene HUETHER III (1900 – 1950)
    Sophia HUETHER (1902 – 1970)
    Eva HUETHER (1904 – 1989)
    Arlene HUETHER (1906 – 2003)
    Jacob HUETHER (1908 – 1966)

Paul Jr.'s (**Barbara's** aunt) sister Maria Barbara Huether married Gottlob Hochstatter in Russia. They immigrated to the United States through Canada and moved to South Dakota. After staying with relatives they moved to Washington State near Black Lake in October of 1902 where they homesteaded 170 acres near Wilson Creek (filed 1903) and about 10 miles northeast of Moses Lake.

Gottlob and Marie's daughter Barbara married Jakob Ottmar. The Ottmar land is located about 12 miles south of the Hochstatter land (Paul Sr. and Paul Jr. are buried in the Ottmar Cemetery).

After the death of his second wife in 1905, Paul Huether Sr. (Barbara's grandfather) moved to the state of Washington to live with his daughter Maria Barbara who was married to Gottlob Hochstatter. Paul Jr.'s son Christ Huether (**Barbara's** brother and Paul Sr.'s grandson) homesteaded 86 acres of land (patent 1920) about 15 miles southeast of the Hochstatter's land.[23]
In 1908 Paul Sr. bought 160 acres of land near Rocky Coulee southeast of Ruff and about 12 miles southeast of the Hochstatter's land and about 2 miles north of his grandson Christ's homestead.

In 1908 Paul Jr. and his family moved by wagon to Washington State to be with Paul's father Paul Sr. In the 1910 Grant County U.S. Census Paul Huether Jr. age 58 and Katherina age 41 are listed as living in Wheeler.[24] Living with Paul and Katherina are son Henry age 20, daughters Caroline age 17, Margrette age 16, **Barbara** age 14, son Andrew age 13, daughter Lydia age 11, son Paul Jr. age 10, daughter Sophia age 8, daughters E. E. (Eva) age 6, and Adeline age 4 and son Jacob S. age 1 and 3 months.

Paul Jr. owned land near Quincy for a time. His son John owned the Idle Hour saloon there before moving to Ruff (see Quincy Chapter for details).

In 1924 Christ Huether bought from Katharina Huether the contents of a hotel located in the town of Ruff, Grant County including the post office fixtures, safe lock boxes and all of the hotel furnishings, a five passenger car engine for a Model 4 T, a Ford Roadster with a truck body, and one half interest in Keystone well drilling outfit consisting of drill, gas engine and all tools.

[23]Christ Huether Homestead, Grant County Final Receipt Vol. B pages 105-106
[24]1910 U.S. CENSUS, Grant County, Washington; Page 270A, image file 0160.tif, Record ID HRP1910GRT5375

Johannes R. HUETHER "John" (Paul Jr.) was born 13 Sep 1879 in Akerman, S. Russia. He died 25 Sep 1924 in Ruff, WA.

John married **Emilie METTLER** "Emilia", daughter of Daniel METTLER and Margarethe HUETHER, on 29 Nov 1914 in Eureka, SD. Emilia was born 3 Sep 1883 in Bridgewater, Dakota Territory. She died 4 Apr 1973 in Bismarck, ND.

They had the following children:

M i **Herbert P. HUETHER** was born 25 Feb 1916 in Grant County, WA. He died Sep 1983 in Riverview, FL.

Herbert married **Bonnie STEELE**. Bonnie was born 5 Mar 1910. She died 17 Oct 1990 in Freeport, IL.

F ii **Ruth E. HUETHER** was born 14 Sep 1917 in Grant County, WA.

F iii **Verna HUETHER** "Peggy" was born 28 Jul 1920 in Grant County, WA.

F iv **Leona Edwina HUETHER** was born 26 May 1922. She died 22 Mar 2000 in Fargo, ND.

Magdalena HUETHER was born 17 Feb 1881 in Paulsthal, S. Russia. She died after 1932 in Spokane, WA.
Aunt Maggie
Magdalena married **Christoph Christian STEINBACH**. Christoph was born 1873 in Odessa, S. Russia. He died after 1932.
They had the following children:

F i **Girl STEINBACH**.

F ii **Girl STEINBACH**.

F iii **Catherine STEINBACH** was born 1901 in Walworth Co., SD. She died 1981 in WA.

F iv **Elizabeth STEINBACH** was born 1902 in Java, SD. She died 1936 in Wenatchee, WA.

M v **Johann STEINBACH** was born 1904 in Town Mountain, SD. He died 1932 in Rattlesnake Flat, WA and was buried in Ritzville Cemetery, WA.

M vi **Christopher Christian STEINBACH** was born 1906 in Ruff, WA. He died 1987 in Green Acres, WA.

M vii **Karl STEINBACH** "Carl" was born 1907 in Ruff, WA. He died 1975 in Green Acres, WA.

M viii **Theodore STEINBACH** was born 1909 in WA. He died 1972 in Spokane, WA.

F ix **Martha STEINBACH** was born 1914 in WA.

F x **Eilesia STEINBACH** was born 1919 in Grant County, WA.

M xi **Robert STEINBACH** was born 1920. was buried 1973.

Christian R. HUETHER "Christ" (Paul Jr.) was born 17 Mar 1885 in Neusatz, S. Russia. He died 15 Nov 1966 in Walla Walla, WA.

His son Herman says that he has Christian's confirmation record with the name spelled Heether at Eureka, SD about 1897. He immigrated in 1890 and received his naturalization in 1912. He was a farmer. Both he and his wife Elizabeth are buried at the IOOF Evergreen Cemetery, Rosalia, WA.

Christ married (1) **Elizabeth HOCHSTATTER**, daughter of Johann Gottlob HOCHSTATTER and Maria Barbara HUETHER, on 5 Jan 1907 in Rathdrum, ID. Elizabeth was born 7 Nov 1887 in Odessa, S. Russia. She died 10 Jan 1949.

They had the following children:

M i **Reinhold Christian HUETHER** "Reinhart" was born 1919 in WA. He died 1954.

M ii **Leo Albert HUETHER** was born 1910. He died 1952 in a railroad accident.

F iii **Elizabeth Lenora HUETHER** was born 4 Aug 1916 in WA. She died 1972.

F iv **Frieda Alviny HUETHER** "Freda" was born 1918 in WA.

M v **Herman HUETHER** was born 1919 in Spokane County, WA.

Christ also married (2) **Lydia (Hoffman) Roloff WEIS** on 1950. Lydia was born 18 Oct 1890 in Kulm, Tarutino, Bessarahia, S. Russia. She died 25 Jan 1983 in Walla Walla, WA.

Heinrich HUETHER "Henry" was born 13 Jul 1889 in Campbell County, South Dakota. He died in 1964 in Walla Walla, WA. Henry R. Huether (2257687) served in the Army in 1918 as a private 1st class and his service was recorded in the Adams County Clerk's Office. It was recorded that he was born in Eureka, So. Dakota.[25]

FILE NO. 35265.

HONORABLE DISCHARGE FROM THE UNITED STATES ARMY

TO ALL WHOM IT MAY CONCERN:

THIS IS TO CERTIFY, That Henry R. Huether 2257687, Private 1st Class, Infantry unassigned, Last Assigned Co. G, 361 Inf. THE UNITED STATES ARMY, as a Testimonial of Honest and Faithful Service, is hereby Honorably Discharged from the military service of the United States by reason of Muster Out Telegram A. G. O. Nov. 16, 1918.

Said Henry R. Huether was born in Eureka, in the State of So. Dakota. When enlisted he was 27 years of age and by occupation a Farmer. He had Brown eyes, Black hair, Dark complexion, and was five feet four inches in height.

Given under my hand at Camp Lewis, Wash. this 1st day of May, one thousand nine hundred and Nineteen.

R. M. Martin
R. M. Martin

Major Infantry, Commanding.

Entitled to Travel Pay to Euphrata, Wash. American Lake, Wash. Offide Camp Supply Depot. Paid Bonus $60.00 Tel. A. G. O. 2-25-19. Paid in Full $102.70.

Frank J. Quinn, Major, Q. M. C.

By Wales M. Signor, 1st Lieut. Inf.

ENLISTMENT RECORD.

Name: Henry R. Huether, 2257687. Grade: Private 1st Class. Enlisted, or Inducted, Sept. 22, 1917, at Euphrata, Wash. Serving in First enlistment period at date of discharge. Prior service: None. Noncommissioned officer: Never. Marksmanship, gunner qualification or rating: Pvt. 1/cl. 013. 1/21/18. Horsemanship: Not Mounted. Battles,

Adams County Miscellaneous Records, Vol. D, pp. 310-311

[25] Adams County Miscellaneous Records, Vol. D, pp. 310-311, Washington State Archives

engagements, skirmishes, expeditions: With A. E. F. from July 6, 1918 to April 15, 1919, St. Mihéal 9/11 - 13/18, Meuse - Argonne 9/26 - 10/12/18, Lys Scheldt, Belgium 10/31 - 11/11/18. Knowledge of any vocation: Farmer. Wounds received in service: None Physical condition when discharged: Good. Typhoid prophylaxis completed Oct. 19,1917. Paratyphoid prophylaxis completed Oct. 19, 1917. Married or single: Single. Character: Excellent. Remarks: No A. W. O. L. Nor Sk. N. L. D. under G. O. 31-1912 or G. O. 45-1914. Entitled to travel pay with 166 D. B. to 10/25/17, Co. G, 361 Inf. to 4/24/19, Casual to date of discharge.

Signature of soldier: Henry R. Huether.

T. L. Kendall,

Captain Infantry

Commanding Disch. Detch., 166 Depot Brigade.

Filed for record this 12th day of May, A. D., 1919 at 8 o'clock and 15 minutes A. M., at the request of Henry R. Huether.

A. C. BANKO, County Auditor.

By [signature] Deputy.

Adams County Miscellaneous Records, Vol. D, pp. 310-311

He was at St. Michael, Meuse – Argonne and Lyn Scheldt, Belgium and had an honorable discharge.

Barbara Huether is covered later in this work in detail.

Margaretha HUETHER (1894 – 1916)

Adam Schatz and Margaret Huether

Paul Eugene Immanuel HUETHER III was born 27 Oct 1900 in Eureka, SD. He died 29 May 1950 in Chewelah, WA.
Buried in Chewelah Pioneer Cemetery, WA
Occupation: Water well driller-contractor
Paul married (1) **Glenna HOYT** on 15 Sep 1924 in Yakima, WA.
They had the following children:

F i **Bernadine Vera HUETHER** was born 21 Jan 1926 in Yakima, WA.

Paul also married (2) **Ruth BLANCHARD** on 1926. Ruth died 25 Nov 1934 in Spokane, WA.
One source says her name is Ruth Genger. Ruth had a son William Tate from a previous marriage. Ruth and their son Robert are buried in Fairmont Cemetery, Spokane.
Paul and Ruth had the following children:

F ii **Pauline Fay HUETHER** was born 2 May 1928 in Cheney, WA.

M iii **Robert HUETHER** was born 8 Apr 1930 in Spokane, WA. He died about 1933.

F iv **Verda Lynne HUETHER** was born 25 Apr 1931 in Spokane, WA.

\+ M v **Paul Eugene HUETHER IV** was born 7 Jan 1934 and died 9 Dec 1990.

After their mother's death Pauline and Verda were placed in foster homes. Paul went to live with the Hayworth family, and Paul's name was changed to Kenneth Hayworth. When Paul was about 8 years old, the Hayworths had a child of their own and sent Paul back to Spokane, Welfare Dept. He and his sisters stayed in the welfare system until they were of age. When he entered the navy, he found out that he had never been legally adopted so he took back his name as Paul Huether IV. He was a yard foreman / served aboard a heavy cruiser June 25, 1951 to Nov. 3, 1954 (USS Helena).
Paul married **Barbara WHITNEY** on 4 Apr 1957. Barbara was born 3 Mar 1937 in Yakima, WA.
They had the following children:

M i **Paul Wallace HUETHER** was born 6 Jul 1957 in Seattle, WA. Died in 2010.

M ii **Kenneth Andrew HUETHER** was born 4 Sep 1958 in Puyallup, WA. Died in 1988.

F iii **Deborah Jean HUETHER** was born 14 Dec 1959 in Auburn, WA

Paul also married (3) **Charlotte PANES** "Lottie" on 2 Jan 1938 in Spokane, WA. Lottie was born 19 Aug 1919 in Republic, WA.
They had the following children:

M vi **Harry George RITTENHOUSE** was born 19 Oct 1942 in Spokane, A.

Harry and his brothers Jerry and Robert were adopted by their stepfather Howard Rittenhouse in 1957. He earned a PhD in biochemistry and does cancer research. His wife has a PhD in biophysics and does cancer research also

M vii **Jerry Thurston RITTENHOUSE** was born 12 Nov 1944 in Tonasket, WA.

M viii **Robert Eugene RITTENHOUSE** was born 8 Feb 1947 in Tonasket, WA

He is an artist and also repairs old fashioned furniture. His wife Yvonne works in an insurance office. Yvonne was Miss Clayton, GA in the 1969 beauty contest and second runner-up to enter Miss Atlanta, GA.

Eva E. HUETHER was born 13 Sep 1904 in SD. She died 27 May 1989 in Opportunity, WA and was buried in Pines Cemetery, Spokane Co., WA.
Eva married **Richard HOEFNER**, son of Henry HOEFNER and Louise OTTMAR, on 1 May 1921. Richard was born 1898 in Herreid, SD. He died 1975 in Spokane, WA and was buried in Pines Cemetery, Spokane Co., WA.
They had the following children:

F i **Iris V. HOEFNER** was born 1921 in Hartline, WA. She died 1981 in Spokane, WA.

M ii **Vinie A. HOEFNER** was born 1922 in Hartline, WA.

F iii **Alma R. HOEFNER** was born 1924 in Hartline, WA.

F iv **Claire F. HOEFNER** was born 1926

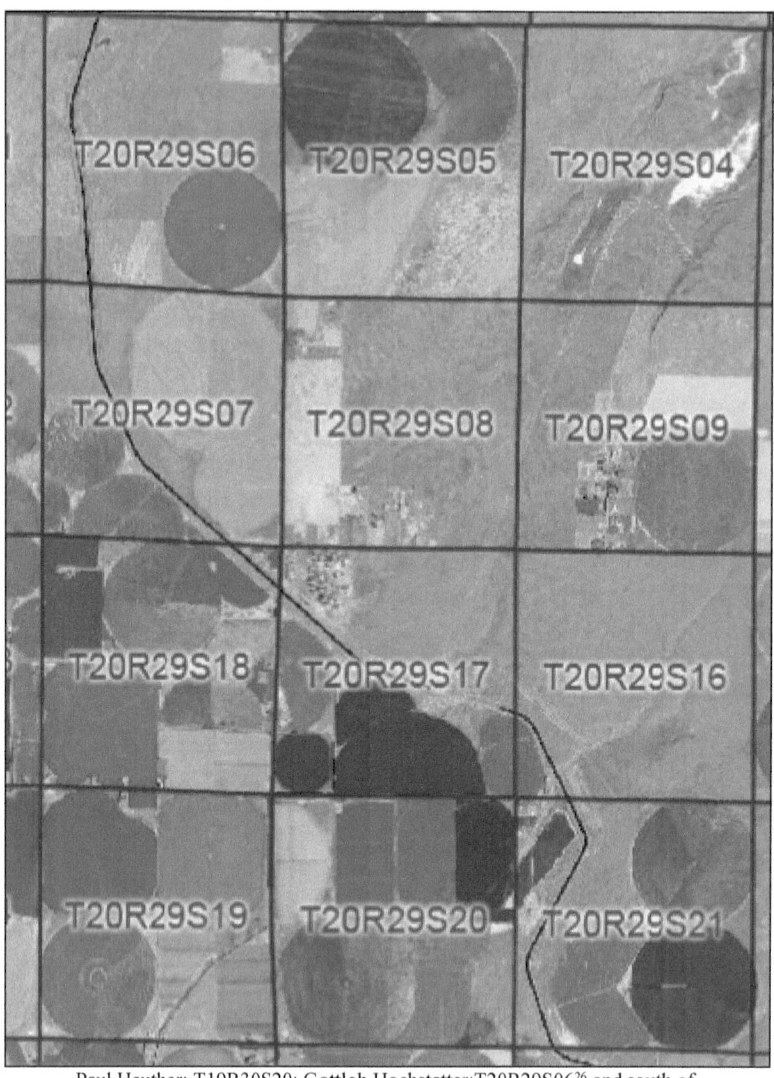

Paul Heuther: T19R30S20; Gottlob Hochstatter:T20R29S06[26] and south of their son John Hochstatter's – near the graveyard at T20R29S26

Johann Gottlob Hochstatter (T20R29S06) is bounded by roads 11 RD NE, 12 RD NE and M RD NE and the canal. The Ottmar cemetery (T20R29S26) is on road P NE and Road 8 NE. Paul Huether's land (T19R30S20) is on Road S NE and Road 2 NE and 3NE.

---

[26] http://grantwa.mapsifter.com/default.aspx

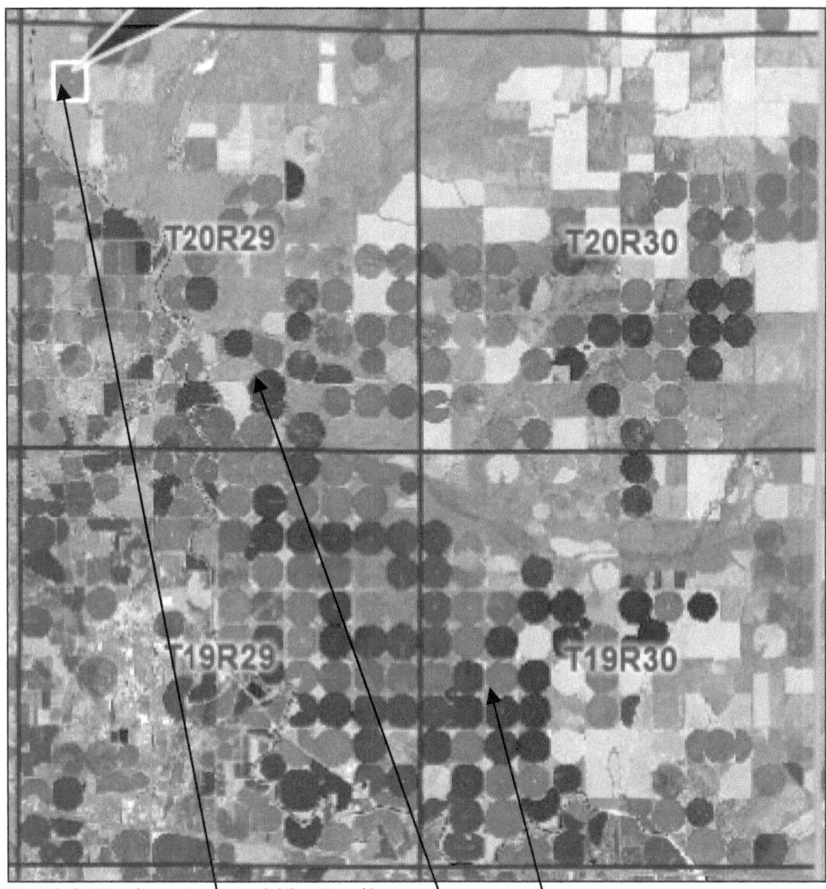

Gottlob Hochstatter would be 3 miles north of the cemetery and the Jocob Ottmar's land. Paul would be 3 miles from the cemetery.

Jacob Ottmar is about 5 miles south of Gottlob Hochstatter and Paul is about 6 miles southeast of Jacob's.

Hochstatter and Huether Ancestral History

This is from the website:

Hochstatter and Huether Ancestral History
Courtesy of Herb Hochstatter, Bakersfield, California
From Germans from Russia Heritage Collection
North Dakota University, Fargo, N.D.
http://library.ndsu.edu/grhc/history_culture/index.html

The section on Johann Hochstatter and Friedricka Luithle and Johann Gottlob Hochstatter and Maria Barbara Huether were printed first in the original but moved to the back in this work to concentrate on Paul Huether, Sr. The section on Gotthold (George) Hochstatter and Alice M. Joyner follows those. The farming methods and stories described in that section would be common to both families.

Paul Jr's sister Barbara had married Johann Gottlob Hochstatter. They homesteaded out in Washington State near Moses Lake. Paul Huether Sr. moved to Washington State after the death of his second wife, in 1905and stayed with the Hochstatters (Barbara was his daughter). In 1908 Paul Huether Jr. and his family moved by wagon to Washington State and settle near relatives Johann Gottlob Hochstatter and his wife Maria Barbara Huether.

Paul Huether, Sr.

Paul Sr. was the sixth child of Johann Ludwig Jacob Huether and Barbara Margareth Zechmeister. He was born 6 Feb 1830 in Peterstal and died on 13 Mar in Eugene OR. He married Maria (Anna) Margaretha Christmann on 25 May 1852 in Freudental. Paul was a shoe maker in Russia.
Paul is listed two places in the Peterstal Liebental District Odessa 1858 census. He is listed in house #23 as a member of Widow Barbara (Zechmeister) Huether's household and his own house #26 with his wife Margaretha and three children. Paul is also listed twice in the Peterstal Liebental District Odessa 1841-1860 Church Family Book. He is listed on page 73 with his wife and five children and page 85 as a member of his mother's family.
Paul and two of his brothers, Ludwig and Simon, immigrated to the United States. Paul and his wife left Neusats, South Russia, where they had moved in 1858 and immigrated to Menno, SD in 1889 before going to Mound City, SD where he homesteaded, they filed claims in Blessing Township, Campbell County, SD.

Paul Huether Sr. b. 6 Feb 1830, Peterstal, m. (1st.) Maria (Anna) Margaretha Christmann, 25 May 1852, Freudental; (2nd.) Louisa (Rosa) Christmann Hettich, about 1891, South Dakota. He died 31 Mar 1930, Eugene OR

Paul and his wife, Maria, had 14 children. My grandmother, Maria Barbara, was their second child. Paul was married twice; there were no children by the second wife. Paul was one of the people instrumental in organizing the Odessa Reformed Church in Sutley, Campbell County, SD. Paul is

listed on the South Dakota 1900 Federal Census as living in Campbell County, Blessing Township.
After the death of his second wife, Louisa (Rosa) Christmann Hettich, in 1905, he moved to the state of Washington to live with family members. Paul's two brothers also homesteaded in SD and remained there until they died.
Maria was born 12 Oct 1832 in Freudental. It is believed that she died in about 1891 in Campbell County, SD. She may be buried in an unmarked grave in the Odessa Reformed Church Cemetery, Sutley, SD. Although according to the Java, SD Centennial Memories, 1900-2000, page 155, Maria and daughter Louise died in 1889 and were buried in Menno, SD.

Paul Huether Jr.

Paul Jr. was born 19 Jan 1853 in Peterstal and died 8 Sep 1918 near Moses Lake, WA. He is buried in the Rocky Coulee, Ottmar Cemetery near Wheeler, WA. The local residents refer to this cemetery as the "Old" Keller Cemetery. Paul married twice, he married Katherina Elisabeth Riedlinger on 27 Dec 1877 in Johannesthal. They had six children.
Katharine was born 18 Dec 1854 in Grossliebental and died in Campbell County, SD on 4 Feb 1892. She left him with six motherless children. Her obituary is listed in "A Collection of Obituaries from Campbell County, SD and southwestern Emmons County, ND," by Bob Dale.
He married Katherine T. Becker 12 Mar 1892 in Campbell County, SD. She was born 23 Sep 1868 in Kassel and died 18 Sep 1948 at Walla Walla, WA. She is buried in the same Cemetery as Paul Jr. They had 10 children.
Paul immigrated to the United States in March 1889 and homesteaded in Campbell County, SD in 1893. He homesteaded Section 14, Township N, Range 75 W. Paul and his family are on the SD 1900 Federal Census and living in Campbell County, SD.
In 1908 Paul and his family moved to Washington State, near Moses Lake. The 1920 Federal Census for Grant County, WA lists the family name as Hertether.

Four generations Back row right-Paul Sr.; left-Paul Jr.; front row right-Christian, son of Paul Jr.; left-Reinhold, son of Christian. Picture taken about 1915.

Paul Jr. with second wife, Katherine T. Becker and family. Back row, L-R; Henry, Chris, John, Magdalene, Katherine, and Rose. Front row, L-R; Caroline, mother Katherine holding Margaret, and Paul Jr. holding Barbara. Paul. b. 19 Jan 1853, Peterstal, d. 8 Sep 1918, near Moses lake WA. Paul married (1st) Katherine Riedlinger, b. 18 Dec 1854, Grossliebental, d. 4 Feb 1892, Campbell County SD, They had 6 children. Married (2nd) Katherine T. Becker, 12 Mar 1892. Campbell County SD, b. 23 Sep 1868, Kassel, d. 18 Sep 1948 Walla Walla WA. They had 10 children. This picture is taken about 1896 or 97 based on how old Barbara appears.

Paul Huether Jr.'s son Christian married into the Hochstatter family.

Continuing from the website:
Hochstatter and Huether Ancestral History
Courtesy of Herb Hochstatter, Bakersfield, California
From Germans from Russia Heritage Collection
North Dakota University, Fargo, N.D.
http://library.ndsu.edu/grhc/history_culture/index.html

Christian Huether
Christian, was born 26 Jan 1885; Nuesatz and died 15 Nov 1956, Walla Walla, WA. He married Elizabeth Hochstatter (my aunt) 5 Jan 1907 at Rathdrum ID. She was born 7 Nov 1887, South Russia and died 10 Jan 1949, Whitman County, WA. They had five children. Both Christian and Elizabeth are buried in the IOOF Evergreen Cemetery, Rosalia, WA. Christian immigrated to the United States in 1890 and received his naturalization in 1912.

Chris and Elizabeth Hochstatter Huether

Maria Barbara Celebrating 90th birthday, 12 Sep 1944. b. 12 Sep 1854, Peterstal, m. Johann Gottlob Hochstatter 7 Nov 1874, Johannestal, d. 10 Oct 1947, Colfax WA

Johann Gottlob Hochstatter

This is from the website:
Hochstatter and Huether Ancestral History
Courtesy of Herb Hochstatter, Bakersfield, California
From Germans from Russia Heritage Collection
North Dakota University, Fargo, N.D.
http://library.ndsu.edu/grhc/history_culture/index.html

Johann Gottlob was born in Alexanderhilf, South Russia 14 Aug 1852. He and his wife immigrated to the U. S. via Canada in the spring of 1902. He left South Russia with his wife and all their children, including two married daughters and one married son, traveling by train and boat to Liverpool, England. On April 1, 1902 they boarded the ship "Lake Ontario" and sailed to Saint John, New Brunswick, Canada, arriving on April, 12. From Saint John they went by train to Winnipeg, Manitoba, then to Java and Kimball, South Dakota. They stayed in South Dakota with relatives during the summer of 1902 and left for the state of Washington in the latter part of October 1902.

The family arrived in Wilson Creek, WA on November 1, 1902, and they lived in a homestead shack during the winter of, 1902-03. Johann filed for homestead rights on March 14, 1903. The homestead was located 10 1/2 miles northeast of Moses Lake. The land description is as follows; Lot one, the south half of the northeast quarter, and the northwest quarter of the southeast quarter of section six in Township twenty north of Range twenty nine east of the Willamette Meridian, Washington, containing 170.35 acres. Patent Number 112198 was issued to him on 17 February 1910 for 170.35 acres of land, permanently giving him this land. You had to pay for any acreage over 160 acres. He paid $2.50 per acre for the excess 10.35 acres. This homestead land remained in the Hochstatter family until it was sold in October 1997. The owners at the time of sale were the three sons of George. None of these sons had any ambition to become farmers or to develop it into smaller farms and then sell them.

They received their mail at the Post Office in Wilson Creek. Later on a country store and post office by the name of Hicksville was started, and in 1910 the post office was moved to Wheeler.

T20R29S06[27]

The first year they grubbed (removed) the sagebrush off of ten acres of their land and four acres off of John Hochstatter's (Johann Gottlob oldest son) place just south of theirs. They borrowed Jacob Ottmar's (Johann Gottlob's son-in-law) plow and harrow. Johann broadcasted the seed by hand. They planted wheat, barley, oats, Russian red wheat, spults, hyssop, and some potatoes and watermelons in their garden. At harvest time Johann cut the grain with a scythe, and raked it by hand with a wooden rake. He shocked the grain in bundles and tied it with straw from the grain. They hauled their water from a well near Black Rock. They watered their garden and filled their cistern with alkali tasting water. Johann had a well drilled in 1907 at a cost of $1,000. When the drillers hit water they lost their tools and spend two weeks trying to fish them out of the well. They weren't successful in retrieving their tools and had to drill another well. The well supplied all of the water they needed and other homesteaders hauled water from it as it was sweeter than the Black Rock water.
After the first year they cleared 80 acres by burning the sagebrush. They bought a John Deere 12 inch gang plow.

[27] http://grantwa.mapsifter.com/default.aspx

George's sister Caroline plowed with a four horse team. Sometimes the sagebrush roots were so strong that they would break the plow blade. In the spring of 1904 they borrowed Ottmar's seeder to plant the 80 acres. In the fall, John and Jacob Ottmar harvested Johann's crop using their header, they put the grain in stacks. Jake Schmauder (another son-in-law of Johann) had a horse driven threshing machine that they used to thrash the grain. Johann Hochstatter got the Schmauders to agree to do the whole harvest for $50. After they arrived for the harvest they tried to talk Johann into paying them seven cents per bushel instead. But he held them to their previous agreement and soothed them with all of the watermelon that they could eat. Fred Schmauder, the youngest one tended the separator. Christian Hochstatter, George's brother and Phillip Gottschalk sewed the sacks after they were filled with the grain.

Johann G. declared his intention to become a Citizen of the United States on 29 September 1902 in Circuit Court, Campbell County, South Dakota. He was naturalized on 13 July 1908 in U. S. District Court, Eastern District of Washington, Spokane. Certification of Naturalization No. 72954 includes the following family members: wife, Barbara; children; Pauline, age 19, Catherine, age 16, and Gotthold, age 10, all of Hicksville, WA.

Johann Gottlob's daughters attended the Keller school, which was built in 1904. They stayed with their oldest sister Barbara, who lived across the road from the school and was married to Jacob Ottmar. The School was located seven miles from the Hochstatter homestead on the northeast corner of where the county roads of 8-N. E. and P-N. E. now intersect.

Most of the above information about Johann Gottlob is from an audio tape by his youngest son Gotthold (George) Hochstatter(my father). The following item appeared in the Dakota Freie Presse on November 11, 1909 and reprinted in the Germans from Russia Heritage Review, No. 20, April 1978.

Washington State Hicksville

"When my wife and I emigrated from South Russia to Washington, disembarking at the station of Wilson Creek, I had no idea where to turn. Since I knew there were already several families from the colony of Neusatz residing here, I

inquired and found they lived 16 miles south of the station. but no one could tell me the exact place since everything here was a virgin land. There were as yet no roads and only occasionally would one find a clapboard shanty on the prairie. However, we finally succeeded in finding our friends Johann and Jakob Ottmar. How awful the landscape looked without grass or vegetation! Often you had to travel four or six miles to get to a well or a low spot for water. Today, however, it looks entirely different. Johann and Jakob Ottmar each have their own houses, large barns and other buildings, a windmill, and orchards and grape vines. Johann Wilging, Jakob and Johann Schmauder, and Ludwig and Johann Flood immigrated into the area from Bessarabia. The latter arrived in 1901. All of them have established themselves beautifully. In the second and third years, schools were built and church services have been conducted in them. Various preachers served the community. Even now we still do not have churches. About 20 miles from us is a Congregational Church and some 14 miles east of Hicksville is another Protestant church which is served by Pastor Stier. Two years ago in Wilson Creek a church was built.
With best regards."

And continues from the website:
Hochstatter and Huether Ancestral History
Courtesy of Herb Hochstatter, Bakersfield, California
From Germans from Russia Heritage Collection
North Dakota University, Fargo, N.D.
http://library.ndsu.edu/grhc/history_culture/index.html

Gottlob Hochstatter

Johann died 27 Jun 1918 at his homestead. He is buried in the Rocky Coulee, Ottmar Cemetery near Wheeler, WA. The local residence refer to this cemetery as the "Old" Keller Cemetery. The location of this cemetery is Township 20 North, Range 29 East, Section 26. Note: His death certificate shows his name as Gotthold, which is incorrect.

He married Maria Barbara Huether on 7 Nov 1874 in Johannesthal, So. Russia. Thirteen children were born to this marriage, ten survived to adulthood. The children are: Johann (1875-1875); Barbara [Ottmar] (1876-1968); Sophia [Arnold] (1877-1956); John D. (1879-1950); Caroline [Greenwalt] (1881- 1956); Karl (1882-xxxx); Christian (1887-1970); Margerethe (1884-1885)l Rosina [Rose] [Dormaier] (1886-before 1941); Elizabeth [Huether] (1887-1949); Pauline [Schaal] (1889-1928); Katherine [Trautman] (1891-1971); and Gotthold [George] (1898-1983) [my father].

Maria was born 12 Sep 1854, Peterstal, South Russia. She died 10 Oct 1947 in Colfax, WA. She is buried in the same Cemetery as her husband Gottlob. Throughout her life she was known as Barbara. It wasn't until I saw her birth record did I realize her name was Maria. She married Frederick Dormaier in 1919 after Johann's death. They had no children. Maria and Frederick had a prenuptial marriage agreement. Maria's father, Paul Huether, Sr., lived to be 100 years old.

Johann Gottlob Hochstatter b. 14 Aug 1852, Alexanderhilf, m. 7 Nov 1874, Johannesthal. d. 27 Jun 1918, on Homestead 12 miles N.E. of Moses Lake, Grant County WA.
Marie Barbara Huether b. 12 Sep 1854, Peterstal, d. 10 Oct 1947, Colfax WA
From the Moses lake Paper: First of the Hochstatters – Johnn Gottlob and his wife Barbara, who homesteaded near Black Lake northeast of Moses Lake posed for this portrait in 1914 near Ruff. They settled at Black Rock in the first decade of this century and founded a family which has been active in this community for more than 60 years. A son, George Hochstatter, was Moses Lake's first fire chief and lives at 314 S. Division St. next to the Sears store.

Johann Gottlob Hochstatter Homestead, Photo taken about 1918-1919. Homestead located 12 miles N. E. of Moses Lake WA. It remained in the family from 1902 until 1997

This is from the website:
Hochstatter and Huether Ancestral History
Courtesy of Herb Hochstatter, Bakersfield, California
From Germans from Russia Heritage Collection
North Dakota University, Fargo, N.D.
http://library.ndsu.edu/grhc/history_culture/index.html

George was the 13th child born to Johann Gottlob and Barbara Huether, ten of the children lived to adulthood. George was born 20 Jul 1898 in Neusatz, South Russia; he died 14 Nov 1983 in Othello, WA. On December 18, 1931 George married Alice Macon Joyner; she was born September 11, 1905 in Steven's County, near Deer Park, WA. Her parents were Samuel Madison Joyner and Core Charlotte Fields. George and Alice raised three sons Herbert George, (me) born at Ritzville, WA, Samuel Francis, born at Ritzville, WA. and the youngest Ellis William, born at Wenatchee, WA. They also have eight grandchildren, two boys and six girls. At the time of George's death there were two great grandsons. They celebrated their Golden Wedding Anniversary on 18 Dec 1981.

George met Alice when she came to work at the Moses Lake Inn for Loren Harris. After they were married, they lived in a house on the west side of the Moses Lake Hardware store on the southeast corner of Broadway and Division Street. In 1939, they purchased a house from Amos Hull, a brother-in-law, and moved in after it had been renovated and updated. When purchased, it had no indoor plumbing. It was located at 314 Germania St., later to be renamed Division St. They lived there until George's death in 1983. Alice moved out in 1984 and sold the place. She moved into an apartment and lived there until her death in 1991.

George started school in the fall of 1908 at the Black Rock School. The Black Rock School was located at the southwest corner of Section 6, Township 20N, Range 29E at present intersection of roads 11 NE and M NE. George's brother John donated the land for the Black Rock School. John D. Hochstatter, Jr. was only five years old but still attended at the same time. The school teachers name was Michaelson. The first school term was for six months and the subsequent terms for eight months. George read the primer in twenty days with his sister's tutoring. Later, more homesteaders came and a school house was built by Charlie Scott, he was from Wilson Creek. The Black Rock School was eventually merged with the Gloyd School. George attended school through part of the 6th grade; the school had no higher grades.

George was more interested in machinery and wheels than class room learning. He bought some books on gas, steam and marine engines and studied them to become a mechanic and operator. He knew that horses were going to be replaced by machines. In 1916 he worked part time for his brother-in-law Christ Dormaier at the Ford garage in Ruff, WA [the Dormaeir family was settled in Quincy]. George worked on the farm and the steam stationary threshing machine. In 1909, George's brother Christ bought a threshing machine. The engine was a thirty-six inch Case, model 2530-25 horsepower engine and a 30 horsepower boiler, with 36 inch drivers on it. In 1919 Christ sold the outfit during harvest and George stayed close to the separator man and learned all he could about the separator and the engine. In 1922 and 1923 George operated the separator and steam traction engine for the new owner and a Holt-Caterpillar for someone else. He took time off from the Minnewash Fish Company to do so. In 1917 George helped a farmer put up hay and cultivate vegetables in Section 14 just east of the town of Nepple. He worked on a gravel crushing crew connecting the Nepple-Ritzville highway. Putting on the first gravel in the summer of 1920. He worked for those contractors for 22 months in eastern Washington. They were laying gravel on highway 2 between Wilson Creek and Marlin in October, 1921. He helped install machinery for the work on the first part of the road fill across Moses Lake. George donated labor on the first fair building that was located in Nepple where the S. E. corner of 5th Ave, and Chestnut Streets are now located. During 1923-24 he operated a launch for the Minnewash Fish Company, while they seined for carp in Moses Lake and shipped, by railroad, forty-six box car loads to the fish market on the east coast. In the fall of 1925 he worked for the Western Cold storage in Nepple, loading apples into box cars. Some years they averaged three thousand car loads of apples. Fresh produce was not available in the stores, so on some weekends during harvest the people from the surrounding counties would drive to Moses Lake to buy fresh vegetables and fruit.

On December 2, 1925, George, his brother John D. and nephew John D., Jr. purchased property from Ed Dry. They were partners in operating the Moses Lake Hardware and M and L Garage for many years until they split the operation in 1944. George operated the hardware store until he sold it in 1955. His nephew operated the garage. His brother John retired from the business. George was a Marshall Wells hardware dealer. The store had a coal burning stove with several chairs around it, and during the winter the old timers would gather around to swap stories.

FILE NO. 46740

BILL OF SALE

KNOW ALL MEN BY THESE PRESENTS, That Edgar Dry the party of the first part, for and in consideration of the sum of Four Thousand and Nine Hundred Thirty Two and 56/100 DOLLARS, to him in hand paid by George G. Hochstatter, John D. Hochstatter and John Hochstatter the parties of the second part, the receipt whereof is hereby acknowledged. does by these presents grant, bargain, sell, convey and confirm unto the said parties of the second part their executors, administrators and assigns, the following described personal property, located and being in Neppel, County of Grant, State of Washington, to-wit: Stock of Hardware and auto supplies, supplies and fixtures.

TO HAVE AND TO HOLD the same to the said parties of the second part, their executors, administrators and assigns, forever.

And the said party of the first part does for himself, his heirs, executors and administrators, covenant and agree to and with the said parties of the second part, their executors, administrators and assigns, to warrant and defend the sale of such property, goods and chattels hereby made unto the said parties of the second part their executors, administrators and assigns, against all and every person and persons whomsoever, lawfully claiming or to claim the same, or any part thereof.

IN TESTIMONY WHEREOF, The said party of the first part has hereunto set his hand and seal this 19th day of November A. D. 1925.

Executed in Presence of:__________ Edgar Dry (SEAL)

STATE OF WASH.)
)ss.
County of Grant)

I, Anna M. Reaugh, a Notary Public in and for said County and State, do hereby certify that on this 19th day of November, A. D. 1925, personally appeared before me Edgar Dry to me known to be the individual described in and who executed the within instrument and acknowledged that he signed and sealed the same as his free and voluntary act and deed, for the uses and purposes therein mentioned.

Given under my hand and official seal this 19 day of November, A. D. 1925.

NOTARY SEAL: ANNA M. REAUGH NOTARY PUBLIC
STATE OF WASHINGTON COMMISSION EXPIRES
MAR. 16, 1927.

Anna M. Reaugh Notary Public.
Residing at Neppel, Wash.

Filed for record on the 20th day of November A.D. 1925 at 15 minutes past 8 o'clock A. M. at the request of George Hochstatter, Neppel, Wash.

W. W. KINSEY, COUNTY AUDITOR
BY Margaret Harris DEPUTY

Adams County, Miscellaneous Records Vol. E, pp. 350-351

George was very active in the Moses Lake civic arena: He was a member of the fair board for three years, 1926-1928; a charter member of the Grant County Historical Society, you can still see some of his donations at the Museum in Ephrata, WA. George also helped organize the Grant County Sportsman Club. Since Moses Lake did not have any game fish in it, in 1927 the state game commission shipped in five and ten gallon cans of bass and they were planted in the lake. Later they planted spiny ray fish that had been seined on the Pend Oreille River. In the 1930's, Frank Bell of Moses Lake and Ephrata became state fish commissioner. He shipped several rail car loads of spiny fish to Moses Lake in care of George. George would then organize other men to pick up the fish and direct them where to plant them in Moses Lake. George liked to fish and enjoyed the shade as he planted a lot of trees along the lake shore. Later the Chamber of Commerce would sponsor a bass fishing contest. He also helped organized the first commercial club of Moses Lake, it was known as the Isaac Walton League and was the fore runner to the chamber of commerce. George and Ed Hull organized the first Boy Scout Troop in Moses Lake in 1931. It was Troop 46, and all three of George's sons were eventual members of this troop.

He was an active member of the Odd Fellows and Rebekah Lodges. While with the Odd Fellows he was active in improvements at Pioneer Memorial Gardens Cemetery, where both he and Alice are buried. In the early to mid-1950's George was active in the Eagles Lodge, cooking for the Saturday night dances and supplying gallons of homemade dill pickles to go with the hamburgers. The cucumbers used in the pickles were from his own garden. After Neppel was incorporated as Moses Lake in 1938, George was selected the first fire chief, and served for four years. In 1958 he was honored for 20 years of service with the fire department. He was a volunteer fireman until retiring in 1965 at age 67, he then became an honorary firemen for life. Before there was a fire department, George's hardware store was about the only place in town that had fire extinguishers. When there was a fire, someone would stop at the hardware store and take the fire extinguishers to fight the fire. Most people did not want to spend the money for a fire extinguisher.

When Moses Lake was incorporated, it did not have any firefighting equipment. Funds were found and George sold Moses Lake six extinguishers at his cost. They were placed throughout town at various businesses. In 1942 when the water mains were installed, the city purchased fire hoses. The volunteer fireman built a hose cart to carry the hose and fire extinguishers. The first fireman to arrive at the station would sound the siren and the first one there with a trailer hitch on their vehicle would hook up the cart and the other men would pile on and off they went to fight the fire. Sometimes the only thing left was the lot where the structure had been standing. Later the first fire truck was purchased with government funds and the generous donations of local merchants who purchased tickets to the annual fireman's ball. At the fireman's ball George was always busy in the kitchen acting as the cook.

During World War II, George and Alice put in 18 hour days in the store. They were busy supplying the needs of the contractors and workers at the Moses Lake Air Base, later it was renamed Larson Air Force Base. They also were supplying the needs of the local farmers and other people in the area. Tools and supplies were scarce and sometimes unavailable because of the war effort.

After George sold the hardware business and moved out in 1955, he worked three summers for the Grant County Housing Authority at the project that was located where McCosh park is now located in Moses Lake. He also kept busy in the summers working in his garden that was located on the N. E. corner of Seventh and Division streets. He always raised more than he and Alice could use and gave away or sold lots of his vegetables, flowers, trees, and shrubs. His vegetables won several blue ribbons at the Grant County Fair. His nursery supplied a lot of the non-fruit trees to Charles Brown, who started the town of George Washington, located southeast of Quincy. As you drive between Moses Lake and Ellensburg on Interstate 90 you can see the size of some of the trees to the south. George was an active bee man, keeping several dozen colonies of bees from which he extracted the honey and sold it. In the winter, George continued repairing oil stoves and furnaces. Marshall Wells had trained him for this in 1927 and had yearly training sessions that he attended. He finally retired for good in 1978 when he was approaching the age of 80.

Gotthold (George) Hochstatter with two horses on the homestead, taken before 1919. George, b. 20 Jul 1898, Nuesatz, Grossliebental. m. Alice Macon Joyner of Deer Park WA, 18 Dec 1931, He. 14 Nov 1983, Othello WA, buried at Moses Lake WA.

In 1957, when his son Sam graduated from Southern California Bible College, George and Alice took their first vacation since being married and attended the ceremony in Costa Mesa, CA. George did not like being idle for long so he helped out by trimming some of the shrubs on the campus.

George was instrumental in organizing the first Hochstatter/Dormaier picnic/reunion in Moses Lake in 1963. In 2003 this gathering celebrated the 40th anniversary of the event. Over the years it has been held in Moses Lake or the Yakima area.

During all these years George leased the Hochstatter homestead, which he had inherited from his mother at the time of her death.

George with four horse team. On the homestead. Taken before 1919.

George and a team of horses. Plowing on the homestead, taken before 1919

George, feeding the chickens. On the homestead, taken before 1919

Christ Hochstatter's threshing crew. Crew posing with cook crew and thrashing machine. Taken before 1919

Christ Hochstatter's threshing crew. Hanging around the cook shack, waiting for lunch. Christ is George's older brother. George is on the far right. Taken before 1919.

Moses Lake Hardware store. Purchased by George, his oldest brother, John, and nephew John Jr. George is standing in front of the store and John Jr. is in front of garage, near the car. George and John Sr. operated the store and John Jr. the garage. George was involved with the store for over 30 years.

Abandoned Hochstatter homestead. Taken sometime in the early 1950's

Hochstatter and Huether Ancestral History

Continuing from the website:
Hochstatter and Huether Ancestral History
Courtesy of Herb Hochstatter, Bakersfield, California
From Germans from Russia Heritage Collection
North Dakota University, Fargo, N.D.
http://library.ndsu.edu/grhc/history_culture/index.html

Reinhold (Rheinhart) Christian Huether
Rhienhold was born in 1909 in Washington state and died 19 Sep 1954, Spokane, Spokane County, WA , buried in Holy Rosary Cemetery, Whitman County, WA. He married Patricia Dowling, and they had five children.

Reinhold (Rheinhart) Christian Huether

Johann Hochstatter and Friedricka Luithle

Johann was born in South Russia 10 Dec 1828; His birth information is based on his age as listed on his death certificate. He is listed on the 1858, 10th census, entry #73, Alexanderhilf, Liebental District, Odessa along with his son Gottlieb (Johann Gottlob). He is listed as age 28 in this census. He came to the US in April 1894; He arrived in New York and went to Java, Walworth County, South Dakota to live with his son Johannes (John). He lived with his son until his death on 21 July 1906. The Walworth County, SD 1900 census for Germans from Russia lists Johann as John, born 1830, immigrated to the U. S. in 1893 and was a widower. He was living with his son John at the time this census was taken.

According to his death record in South Dakota, he is buried in the Congregational Cemetery five miles north of Java, SD. This location would put his grave near the Walworth and Campbell County line.

He was married to Friedricka Luithle, her death registration lists him as her spouse. Date of marriage in unknown. She was born 10 June 1831 in Marienfeld, South Russia and died 22 January 1869 in Neusatz, South Russia. Her birth is based on age listed on the death register. She is listed in the 1858 census for Grossliebental and Alexanderhilf. Daughters Karolina and Dorothea (Entzy) are also listed in the Alexanderhilf census. Friedricka age is listed as 24.

I have been able to identify nine children born to this marriage. Johann (1850-1850), Johann Gottlob (1852-1918) [my line], Karoline (1855- xxxx), Dorothea (1857-xxxx), Katharine (1859-1860), Christian (1861- 1909), Jacob (1863-1863), Jacob (1864-1865), and Johannes [John] (1867-1943).

Johann Hochstatter b. 10 Dec 1828, Grossliebental, m. abt. 1849. d. 21 Jul 1906, Walworth County SD. Friedricka Luithle b. 10 Jun 1831, Marienfeld. d. 22 Jan 1869, Nuesatz, Grossliebental

Johann Hochstatter daughter, Dorthea & family
Dorthea, b. 29 Jul 1857. Grossliebental. m. Christian Entzi 10 May 1876, Johannestal. Young girl believed to be daughter of Dorthea & Christian, name unknown.

John Hochstatter

The Story of John Hochstatter
The Dam Was a Dream but He Bought a Ticket
By Dorothy Garlinghouse[28]

The price of the ticket was one dollar. It was for a dream. And in the 1920s a dollar was a lot of money for any commodity, but the people of the Columbia Basin area bought a lot of those tickets, because they believed in their dream. Enough of them were sold to finance James O'Sullivan's trips to Washington where he convincingly told about the people's vision of irrigation for this arid expanse by means of a huge dam, the proportions of which were unheard of in the history of engineering.

John Hochstatter still has one of those tickets among his souvenirs, for he was well aware of the almost insurmountable obstacles confronting farmers here during the dry land years. His parents homesteaded near Gloyd in 1902, "on the highest spot in the area" where John helped farm their 800 acres until they came to Moses Lake in 1925.

His desire to work with automatics increased as he took correspondence courses in that field when he wasn't cleaning wheat with gasoline-run engines, or doing other farm chores. He became fascinated with electronics in 1921, when the first power lines went in, and recalls that before that time Neppel had its own power plant and was very proud of her street lights.

Ramona Busher became his wife in 1930 and four children were born to them. Their two sons, Dan and Ben, now help their father full time with his electrical repair and motor winding business.

After the war Hochstatter ran the garage that had been in conjunction with the Edgar Dry Hardware Store, which he and his uncle had bought many years before.

"The hardware store's fire extinguishers were about the only firefighting equipment in town during that time," he said, "and they saved the hotel several times.

He served on the first volunteer fire department when the only equipment was a trailer with some hoses on it. The

[28] CBM, Moses Lake, Wash., Aug. 9, 1963,Page C-8

contraption was simply hooked onto any car available at the time of a fire that had a trailer knob on it. He remembers the "OCD" (Office of Civil Defense) pumps that pumped water from the lake as the first real equipment they had.

Some years later he built an electrical shop where the Fidelity Savings & Loan building is now. As he told of its construction, he recalled that the present Eagles building contains some of the lumber from the one-room schoolhouse he attended at Black Rock.

Lumber was scarce as rain and none of it that could be re-used was ever wasted. The nostalgic look backward gave way to talk about the old pot-bellied stove that warmed the school and half frozen children who had to walk many miles for a meager education.

Green was a rare color in this desert. Grass and trees were almost non-existent. The first project undertaken by the Lions Club, of which Hochstatter is a charter member, was to put in the pipes in preparation for a park where the library is now.

Lions are not allowed to own the buildings in which they meet, so in order to have a meeting place, several members called themselves the "Purple Sage Club" and bought one of the buildings used for a labor camp while Larson Air Force Base was being built during World War II.

Long hours of working and planning left little time for recreation, but when it came it was doubly enjoyed. Home-made ice cream was in abundance at Sunday picnics that brought neighbors for miles around.

They fished for carp to be smoked in their smokehouse where mouth-watering bacons and hams were processed, but John was careful to point out that the fish and pork "were not prepared in there at the same time."

Carp for this purpose were caught mostly in the winter months when the edges of ice on Crab Creek left a small stream running through its channel. This made the fish easy to catch. Lake carp were caught in abundance, however, and placed in the ice house until they were shipped to the east for Jewish celebrations feasts.

Just after the war Hochstatter organized the Aero Club for the purpose of building runways for private planes and sold 40 shares of stock at $25 a share, which were all paid off this year.

He kept close watch on the progress of the area and had close contact with its development during the 10 years he served on

the city council. He says the growth and population gains far exceeded his expectations.
"Farming will continue to be the basic economy," he commented.
His life continues to be filled with work and pleasure. His business keeps him occupied most of the time, but travel is a never-ending means of marvel to him, and his file of interesting pictures he took in Europe last year testifies to what he calls "the most interesting highlight of my life."

George Hochstatter

Wreckers Demolish Old City landmark
By Paul George
September 25, 1956
Down it goes – The Hochstatter Building, a 44 year-old structure in downtown Moses Lake is being torn down. Built in Wheeler in 1912 it was moved to its present site in 1922. – Herald photo.

An old two-story frame building, almost as old as Grant County and a landmark in the true sense of the word, is being demolished today.
The Hochstatter Building in the 100 block of East Broadway in downtown Moses Lake was being ripped apart by John D. Sooter of Cascade Valley. A Portland woman, owner of the building and property, has not announced plans for any new construction on the lot.
An explanation of why the structure is truly a landmark comes from George Hochstatter, a 58 year old Moses Lake pioneer who owned and operated the building and the Moses Lake Hardware store housed there for almost 30 years.
Hochstatter said the building is situated on a four section corner and engineers surveying near Moses lake would "sight in" on the chimney of the building. Because of its location the building is really "the hub of the old town of Neppel."

Built at Wheeler
A plat recorded in 1912 laid out the downtown section of what is now Moses Lake. When the community incorporated in 1938, the name Moses Lake replaced Neppel.

The structure was built in Wheeler by the Wheeler Mercantile Co. in 1912, three years after Douglas County was split to form Grant County.

Two homesteaders, Lumbquist and Westfield, owned Wheeler Mercantile Co., containing the telephone exchange, a grocery store and hardware store. Gus Westfield and wife, Phoebe, operated the business until 1918 when it failed and was purchased by Ed Dry.

Moved in 1922

Dry operated the Wheeler Hardware store in the building until 1922 when the structure was hauled five miles to Moses Lake and set down on its present site.

At that time, Hockstatter said, there were about six buildings in what is now downtown Moses Lake. One was the Moses Lake State Bank, a building which housed the Wheeler State Bank when it was located in Wheeler.

Presently, this building contained part of the McInroy Meat Co. on Valley road. Besides several residences, another prominent building was the community hall, built where the Shoe Box is presently situated on Broadway and Ash Streets.

Opened in 1925

At 2 p.m. Nov. 17, 1925, George Hochstatter, his brother Johann and their nephew John D. Hochstatter opened the Moses Lake Hardware Store in the building.

Hochstatter sold the business and stock Aug. 14, 1955. "I just got tired of it," he said. He now operates a small fixit shop in the garage of his home, 314 Division Street, next door to the post office.

"We fix everything but broken hearts," was the motto of the old Moses Lake Hardware store. Besides general hardware department, it contained a general repair service.

At one time it employed eight persons besides George and his wife, Alice. George ran the business by himself after 1944 when the partnership dissolved.

An old timer in the basin, Hochstatter is the son of a couple who homesteaded near Wilson Creek in 1903. The year before they had immigrated to the United States from Southern Russia near the Black Sea, where George was born.

Descendants of Ludwig HUETHER - Third Generation

16. **Maria Barbara HUETHER** (Paul, Ludwig Jacob) was born 24 Sep 1854 in Peterstal, S. Russia. She died 10 Oct 1947 in Colfax, Washington.
Maria married **Johann Gottlob HOCHSTATTER**, son of Johann HOCHSTETTER and Fredricka LUITHLE, on 7 Nov 1874 in Johannesthal, S. Russia. Johann was born 14 Aug 1852 in Grossliebental, S. Russia. He died 27 Jun 1918 in on the homestead near Moses Lake, Washington.
They had the following children:

	45 M	i	**Johann HOCHSTATTER** was born 11 Jul 1875 in Neusatz, S. Russia. He died 17 Jul 1875 in Neusatz, S. Russia.
+	46 F	ii	**Barbara HOCHSTATTER** was born 1876 and died 1968.
	47 F	iii	**Sophia HOCHSTATTER** was born 1877 in Neusatz, South Russia. She died 1956 and was buried in Mountain View Cemetery, Tacoma, WA.
	48 M	iv	**Johann HOCHSTATTER** "John D." was born 1879 in Neusatz, South Russia. He died 5 Jan 1948 in Moses Lake, WA.
	49 F	v	**Corolina HOCHSTATTER** was born 1881. She died 1956.
	50 M	vi	**Christian HOCHSTATTER** was born 1883 in Russia. He died 1970 in Yakima, WA.
	51 F	vii	**Margarethe HOCHSTATTER** was born 1884. She died 1885.
	52 F	viii	**Rosina HOCHSTATTER** "Rose" was born 1886. She died bfr 1941.
	53 F	ix	**Elizabeth HOCHSTATTER** was born 1887 in Russia. She died 1949.
	54 F	x	**Pauline HOCHSTATTER** was born 1889. She died 1928 in Odessa, WA.
	55 F	xi	**Katherine HOCHSTATTER** was born 1891. She died 1971 in Yakima, WA.
	56 M	xii	**Gotthold G. HOCHSTATTER** "George" was born 1898. He died 1983 in Othello, WA.

Barbara Sophia Huether Hockstatter

Barbara Huether Hockstatter's three children

Descendants of Ludwig HUETHER - Fourth Generation - Ottmar

46. **Barbara HOCHSTATTER** (Maria Barbara HUETHER , Paul , Ludwig Jacob) was born 1876 in Neusatz, South Russia. She died 1968 in Lincoln Co., WA.
Barbara and Jacob Ottmar came to Grant County, WA before her parents and the rest of the children. She and her husband are buried in Odessa, WA.
Barbara married **Jakob OTTMAR** on 1897. Jakob was born 1874 in Neusatz, S. Russia. He died 1954 in Odessa, Washington.
They immigrated April 1902 and homesteaded near Wheeler, WA. It is reported that he had Parkinson's from his mid to late thirties. His boys were the farmers with him directing the work. He was a businessman and very organized but had no strength to work. He was bedfast for 14 years, and his wife took care of him until he died. They were devoted to each other.

Jakob and Barbara had the following children:

65 M i **Jacob OTTMAR** was born 1897. He died 1910 in Hicksville (Moses Lake), WA.
66 M ii **John OTTMAR** was born 1899. He died 1965 in Colfax, WA.
67 F iii **Barbara OTTMAR** was born 1901. She died 1964 in Lind, WA.
68 M iv **Christian OTTMAR** was born 1903.
69 F v **Christina OTTMAR** was born 1904. She died 1904.
70 F vi **Margaret OTTMAR** was born 1906.
71 M vii **Jacob OTTMAR** was born 1908.
72 F viii **Pauline OTTMAR** was born 1909.
73 M ix **Whilhelm OTTMAR** was born 1911.
74 M x **Benjamin OTTMAR** was born 1913.
75 M xi **Reinhold OTTMAR** was born 1915.
76 F xii **Eleanor OTTMAR** was born 1918. She died 1922.

Ottmar

Christ Huether testified to the clerk on the Ottmar's behave in the transfer of land in 1915. The land transferred a homestead from John W. Hickman to Jacob Ottmar in 1915.

FILE NO. 24002.

State of Washington)
: ss.
County of Grant.)

Christ Hochstatter being first duly sworn, on oath deposes and says: That he is well and personally acquainted with John W. Hickman, who acquired title, by United States Patent dated October 20, 1910, to the following described real estate in the County of Grant State of Washington:

The South half of the Northeast quarter and the south half of the Northwest quarter of Section Twenty-six, Township Twenty North, Range Twenty-nine East of the Willamette Meridian:

Also that he is personally well acquainted with J. W. Hickman who with his wife Sarah Hickman conveyed the above described real estate to Jacob Ottmar by Warranty Deed dated February 2, 1915.

That he knows of his own personal knowledge that the said John W. Hickman and the said J. W. Hickman is one and the same person.

Christ Hochstatter.

Subscribed and sworn to before me this 20th. day of April, A. D. 1915.

J. E. Bassett.

Notary Public in and for the State of Washington, residing at Wheeler, Grant County, Washington.

Notary Seal J. E. Bassett.
Commission expires Jan 10, 1919.

Filed for record at request of Grant Douglas Abst Co. 8 day of June A. D. 1915, at 4 o'clock and 5 minutes p.m.

C. T. Sanders, County Auditor.
By Imanuel Sieler ..... Deputy.

Adams County Miscellaneous Records Volume C, pages 418-419

Paul Huether Jr.'s Grave

Author at Paul Huether's Grave near Moses Lake July 8, 2011

Paul Huether Jr., and Katherine (Becker) Huether, Barbara's parents are buried in the Rocky Coulee, Ottmar Cemetery, Grant County, Washington (T20N R29E, Section 26). It is also known as the old Keller Cemetery by locals. The cemetery began when a Mr. Ottmar donated one acre of land to the Evangelical Church in Ruff about 1910.

To reach the Rocky Coulee, Ottmar Cemetery from I90 in Moses Lake, take the Highway 17 cut-off north toward Ephrata. About 2 miles, take a right at the Wheeler Road – this turns into Road 3 NE. Go a couple miles and just past the irrigation canal turn left onto O NE and travel north.

Stay on the pavement for about a mile and turn right onto Road 6 NE (going east) for about a mile and then left onto P NE (going north again) up a long hill. At the top of the hill is the intersection of Road P NE and Road 8 NE. The cemetery is at the south east corner of the intersection and has a white gate.

Paul Huether Sr. and his wife Katherine are also buried in the Ottmar Cemetery in unmarked graves.

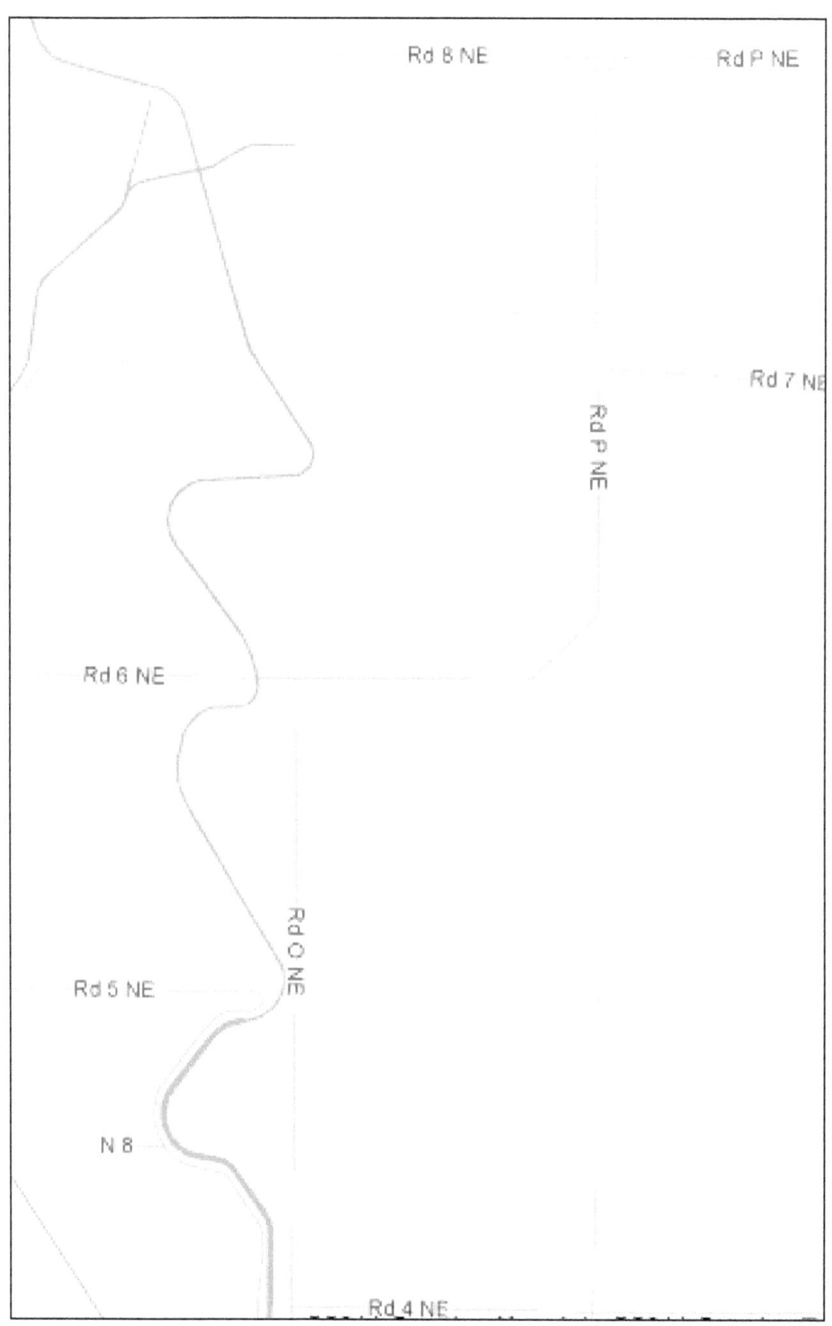
Rd 8 NE
Rd P NE
Rd 7 NE
Rd P NE
Rd 6 NE
Rd O NE
Rd 5 NE
N 8
Rd 4 NE

The Cemetery itself commands a wonderful panoramic view of the entire area as it is located at the top of a hill. The grounds are flat and very overgrown with weeds.

Arial map of Wheeler, note two irrigation circles are about 1 mile.

Several graves are Hochstatter. Sophia (1822 -) and John Hochstatter (1879 – 1948) and Barbara (1854-1947) and Gottlob Hochstatter (1852-1918).

Gate into Rocky Coulee, Ottmar Cemetery, aka Old Keller Cemetery entrance, 2011

From inside the gate looking southwest, the far stone in the grass is Huether, 2011

Huether stone looking back toward gate, 2011

Great view looking southwest from stone, 2011

Large headstone with white rock border behind it. At base of headstone is family name of **Huether**- German inscription:
Hier Ruht in Dem Herren Jesu Christi Paul Huether Geboren Den 31 Jan 1853 Gestboren Den 8 Sept 1918
Der Herr ist Mein Hirteetc Katherine Psalm 28 Sept 23, 1868 Sept 18, 1948

HIER RUHT IN DEM
HERRN JESU CHRISTI
PAUL HUETHER
GEBOREN DEN 31. JAN. 1853
GESTORBEN DEN 8. SEPT. 1918
DER HERR IST MEIN HIRTE ETC
KATHERINE T.
HUETHER

Maria Barbara Huether Hochstatter (Dormaier) Funeral
These are her children:
Elizabeth, Sophia, Christian, Carolina, George, Barbara, John D., Katherine

Chapter 6 – John Nagel and Barbara Huether

This is taken from notes with Edna Emmick on 1/14/2000 and 6/11/2000.

Barbara Huether

Barbara Huether was born in Sutley, South Dakota. Barbara's family had moved from South Dakota on a wagon when she was eight to Rocky Coulee near Moses Lake in Grant County (then Douglas County), Washington. Her dad, Paul, was a farmer. He cut himself and got blood poisoning and died in 1918 when he was about 65. John Nagel, who Barbara would marry, was working as a hired hand nearby. He was buying his own land and knew how to farm and so was considered a good catch.

John Nagel

Born 1883, February 27th(?), fought in the Japanese and Russian War. In Manchuria he was told the war was over and you can go home. By the time they got home, the revolution had started and he was to be drafted again so his family gathered up money and his brother's passport and he came to Washington State in 1911 (through Canada or maybe Ellis Island?). His mother's name was Elisabeth. He had some sisters that came to Canada, he thought, but never heard more. He once, late in life, asked to be taken to Canada to find his sisters not realizing how large Canada was. The Huethers knew him as a distant relative, 4th cousin or so through Barbara's mother's side (the Beckers). He may have gone first to South Dakota before coming to Washington.

There are multiple land transactions for a Frederick (or Fred) R. Nagel (or Nagle) and his wife, Georgia Alice Nagel, from Twin Falls, Idaho in Grant County records from 1909 into the 1920s (some in the town of Neppel – Moses Lake). He was active buying and selling land. This is a possible relative and maybe why John Nagel came out to Washington but no mention in family history has a named Nagel relative in Washington so this connection is very speculative.[29]

In the 1920 Adams County U.S. Census John Nagel (listed as Nagle) age 35 is head of household, born in Russia, immigrated in 1911 and naturalized in 1917. His wife Barbara age 25 born in South Dakota is listed with sons John age 2 years and Carl age 8 months.[30]

---

[29] Grant County Warranty Deed Book Vol. 1, page 227 and WD Book Vol. 19 page 485.

[30] 1920 U.S. CENSUS, Adams County, Washington; Copyright 2001,Eugene Jenkins, 1381 Longmire Lane, Selah, WA 98942; jenkinsgen@nwinfo.net, http://www.webbitt.com/volga/WA-adams-cty.txt

In the 1920 Grant County U.S. Census Katherina is listed as head of household (Paul Jr. had died earlier) age 51. Living with her was Paul Sr. age 89 (the name is spelled Herether in the records) listed as born in Russia, immigrated in 1890 and naturalized in 1895. Listed with her are son Andrew age 23, Lydia age 21 (she is mentioned in the Nagel stories), Paul age 19, Sofia age 17, Eva age 15, Adeline age 13, and Jacob age 11.[31]

Also in Grant County in 1920 is listed John Hochstatter age 40 born in Russia, immigrated in 1902 and naturalized in 1909, with his wife Rosa age 37 and their children, Benjamin age 20, John D. age 16, Christian age 15, Berther age 12, Emma age 12, Sofa age 10, Magdelena age 8, Rienhold age 6, Clara age 4 and Feda age 2 months. Gotthold Hochstatter age 21 is listed as his own head of household.[32]

John and Barbara Nagel

John and Barbara married on March 15th, 1917 and settled near Lind on a purchased farm. Edna was born in Lind and then moved to Spangle, Newman Lake and later to Rathdrum.

From Kathy:

> I visited my brothers recently and talked to them about our grandfather. Bob thinks John's real name was Carl. John, my brother, says his mother's name was Elizabeth. No last name. I am sure there is an Ellis Island ID somewhere that would be of great help to us. Bob said he was a Kazaks, the personal soldiers of the Czar.

From Janet:

> Anyway, yes Grandpa was born in Germany, emigrated to Russia when the Czar offered free land to young men, only to find out Czar wanted able bodied men to send to war so Pop took his brother's name and came to America to avoid fighting in the war for Russia. Cousin Kathy has checked into some of this as well.

---

[31] 1920 U.S. CENSUS, Grant County, Washington; Copyright 2001,Eugene Jenkins, 1381 Longmire Lane, Selah, WA 98942; jenkinsgen@nwinfo.net, http://www.webbitt.com/volga/WA-grant-cty.txt

[32] 1920 U.S. CENSUS, Grant County, Washington; Copyright 2001,Eugene Jenkins, 1381 Longmire Lane, Selah, WA 98942; jenkinsgen@nwinfo.net, http://www.webbitt.com/volga/WA-grant-cty.txt

Descendants of Ludwig HUETHER - Fourth Generation

Family Tree Fourth Generation

Barbara HUETHER (1895 – 1994)
John NAGEL (1883 – 1962)
- John NAGEL Jr. (1918 – 1975)
- Carl NAGEL (1919 – 1991)
- Gertie NAGEL (1921 – 2005)
- Anna NAGEL (1923 -)
- **Edna Ottile NAGEL** (1925 – 2010)
- Harold NAGEL (1927 – 2005)
- Dorothy NAGEL (1929 -)
- Herbie NAGEL (1931 -)

---

31. **Barbara HUETHER** (Paul , Paul , Ludwig Jacob) was born 23 Aug 1895 in Sutley, SD. She died 3 Jul 1994 in Rathdrum, ID.

Barbara married **John NAGEL**, son of Elizabeth, on 15 Mar 1917. John was born 28 Feb 1883 in in Russia. He died in 1962 in Rathdrum, ID.

They had the following children:

	57	M	i	**John NAGEL Jr.** was born 25 Jan 1918 in Lind, WA. He died 21 May 1975. John married (1) **Anna Laura HARMS** on 8 Nov 1941. Anna was born 4 Nov 1922. She died 23 Dec 1960. John also married (2) **Helen JONES**.
+	58	M	ii	**Carl NAGEL** was born 11 Jun 1919 and died 5 Nov 1991.
+	59	F	iii	**Gertrude Lydia NAGEL** was born 28 May 1921 and died 17 Feb 2005.
+	60	F	iv	**Anna Freida NAGEL** was born 27 Mar 1923.
+	61	F	v	**Edna Ottile NAGEL** was born 12 Oct 1925 and died 13 Aug 2010.
+	62	M	vi	**Harold NAGEL** was born 19 Apr 1927 and died 26 Feb 2005.
+	63	F	vii	**Dorothy Madeline NAGEL** was born 9 Jul 1929.
+	64	M	viii	**Herbert NAGEL** was born 19 Aug 1931.

Lind

Lind Family Stories

My mom, Edna remembers that her father John would save his money and buy land next to him as it became available. John Nagel had the farm mortgaged; he owned two sections of dry wheat land and had a Buick car. They were doing well financially. In 1929, he had a crop failure and couldn't pay the mortgage. John took the best horses to Barbara's sister (aunt Lydia) to hide from the creditors. It was a Jew that ran the bank and foreclosed on the farm. John never used the word Jew again, but always said "damnjew." Edna didn't realize that the single word Jew existed until she was about 15 years old.

Edna has a plate in her dining room that is part of the set Barbara received when she got married in 1917.

John farmed with eight to twelve horse teams to pull the combine. He was a good horse trader and refused to move to tractors. He had to have a pair or matched set on the teams. If one horse was white, he would look all over to find another white horse to pair on the team.

When asked how many kids he had, John used to say -- "about two and a half dozen". They had eight kids which would be half a dozen and two. When asked how he fed them all, he would say "they just eat one meal a day, start in the morning and finish at night."

One of Edna's earliest memories is seeing Dorothy on the floor at about eight months old. John would feed her wine, and she got real sick and was on the floor on a blanket.

Before moving from Lind, the house was very big and had an upstairs. The family that bought the farm lived in the upstairs for a while until the Nagel family moved out. The lady upstairs, took a liking to Dorothy (about two) and would come down stairs and get her. Edna would ask mother where Dorothy was and Barbara would say outside. Edna would go out onto the porch and call and call and sit on the porch crying for her.

When Edna was four years old in Lind she could sing Jesus loves me in German. She used to sing it before she got her Christmas candy and would cry each time.

Papa drove into Lind one day. The car had suicide doors. Anna told Edna that the door wasn't closed tight. Edna went to close the door and the door swung out with her. It scared the hell out of papa John.

Papa rolled his own cigarettes with Prince Albert pipe tobacco and smoked constantly.

Johnnie and Charlie, Gertie and Anna, Edna and Harold
About 1928 in Lind House in background

The family went to the mission prairie school with just one teacher for all eight grades. The kids would cut through the field to get to the school instead of going on the road. Edna, being small, couldn't keep up. There was a big ditch with snow run off and the big kids would jump over it, but Edna fell in.

Anna and Gertie played together, but wouldn't let Edna play with them because Mother would ask Edna what they had done, and Edna would tell on them. They would do everything to avoid her. Edna had a cat that looked like an orange tiger. It went out to play with Gertie and Anna. The cat was walking on the rail fence and Gertie said "better run to the house because there's a tiger" and Edna went running to the house balling because she believed her. This is Gertie's favorite story -- "there's a tiger".

Anna, Edna and Gertie, About 1929
Taken in Lind, on the farm, Barn in back on left

The toilet was an outhouse. Before Edna went to school while the other kids were in school, Mama and Papa were busy patching wheat sacks and couldn't take Edna out to the toilet. Edna got half way out to the toilet and the Great Dane behind the toilet stood up and started yawning. Edna screamed and Mama and Papa came running out.

Anna, Edna and Gertie, taken same day
Lind, about 1929, in front of house
The dog would take her puppies under the porch

There were always dogs around the house. Papa would send Harold under the house when he was 3 or 4 years old to get the puppies and Papa would kill them (too many dogs). He told Harold he could have the one he wanted; Edna remembers Harold sobbing and jumping up and down screaming when papa killed the puppies.

They had a horse named Peenie. She was a very gentle horse and had a colt named Betsy. Edna considered Betsy to be her horse. The kids could walk under Peenie and squeeze horse milk into their mouths. The kids would climb all over her.

East of the mountains, the tumbleweeds are huge. The kids would tie a rope to the tumbleweeds and the wind would blow them across the prairie hanging onto the rope.

The one room schoolhouse had a library store room. Edna went in to get some paste and the push lock closed and Edna got locked in. She started crying. The teacher couldn't tell her how to open the lock so one of the eight-grade boys crawled in the windows to unlock it.

In Lind, Charlie and Johnny and Gertie and Anna got small pox vaccinations, Edna cried because she didn't get one. Anna said she'd vaccinate her, got the hot stove poker from the stove and burned Edna's arm.

Lind Land Legal Descriptions

John Nagel married Barbara Huether on March 15th, 1917 and settled near Lind on a purchased farm. John purchased the land from James Neilson in November of 1917.[33] This was the North half of Southeast quarter and North Half of the Southwest quarter of Section 10 Township 15 Range 33.

215 **The Grantor** Lucy Neilson and James Neilson, her husband
of Spokane County of Spokane State of Washington for and in consideration of
Six Thousand Four Hundred DOLLARS,
in hand paid, convey and warrant to Johan Nagel, Lind, Wash.
the following described real estate, situated in the County of Adams, State of Washington,
The North Half of the Southeast quarter (N½ of SE¼) and the North Half of the Southwest quarter (N½ of SW¼) of Section Ten (10) in Township Fifteen (15) North of Range Thirty-three (33) E W M. containing 160 acres more or less according to the government survey.

Dated this 30th day of October A.D. 1917

Lucy Neilson (Seal)
James Neilson (Seal)

STATE OF WASHINGTON, County of Spokane ss. I, the undersigned, a Notary Public in and for the State of Washington do hereby certify that on this 30th day of October 1917 personally appeared before me Lucy Neilson and James Neilson, her husband to me known to be the individuals described in and who executed the within instrument, and acknowledged that they signed the same as their free and voluntary act and deed for the uses and purposes therein mentioned.

Given under my hand and official seal this 30th day of October A.D. 1917

SEAL

J. C. Farrington
Notary Public for State of Washington, Residing at Spokane, Washington

Filed for record this 28 day of Nov. A.D. 1917 at 4:30 o'clock [illegible]M.
Laura Schragg Auditor.
By [illegible] Deputy.

The Granter Lucy Nelson and James Nelson, her husband of Spokane County convey to Johan Nagel, Lind, Washington in consideration of $6,400 the North Half of the Southeast Quarter and the North Half of the Southwest Quarter of Section ten in township fifteen north of range thirty-three (Section 10, Township 15, Range 33 containing 160 acres dated October 30, 1917. Book 39 page 215;
*Nov. 28, 1917 Grantee Nagel, Johan; Grantor James Neilson et ux; Warranty Deed; Book 39 page 215; N2 SE4 & N2S104 10 15 33

[33] Original purchase from James Neilson: *Nov. 28, 1917 Grantee Nagel, Johan; Grantor James Neilson et ux; Warranty Deed; Book 39 page 215; N2 SE4 & N2S104 10 15 33; Index To Deeds, Adams County, Washington (Buying) see document.

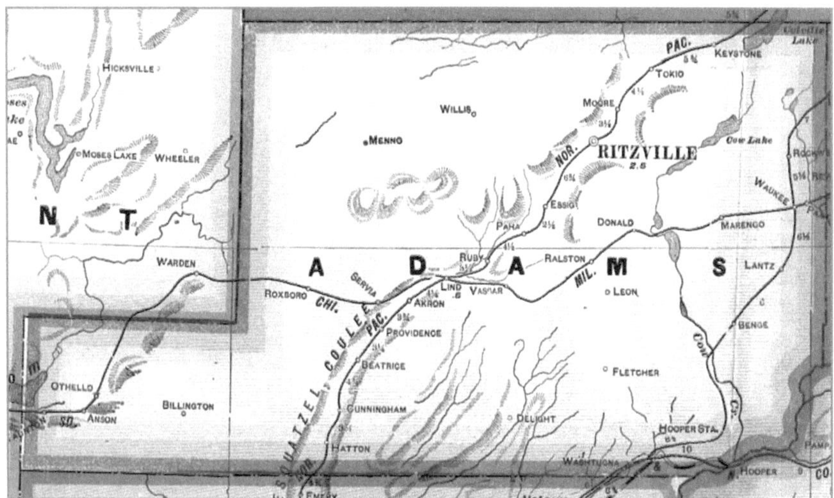

1909 Map of Adams County

The land is located about 12 miles south of Lind near the Cunningham railroad junction.

In 1919 John made an agreement with Jacob Kasper to purchase the adjacent land (North half South half of T15R33S10) which he paid off in 1924.[34]

[34] Agreement with Kasper on adjacent land: Sept. 3, 1919 Grantor Nagel, Johann et. ux; Grantee William Kasper; GCH; Recorded Book 53 page 71; Description: N2 S2 of 10 15 33; General Index – Direct, Adams County, Washington, (Selling)
Buying adjacent land from Kasper: June 13, 1924 Grantee Nagel, John; Grantor William Kasper et. un; G.C.D; Book 53 page 482; description: N2 S2 of 10 15 33; General Index – Reverse, Adams County, Washington, (Buying) See document.

BOOK 53 Quit Claim Deed Pg 71

#11860

THIS INDENTURE, Made the 30th day of August, 1919 in the year of our Lord one thousand nine hundred and nineteen,

BETWEEN Johan Nagel and Babara Nagel, his wife

the parties of the first part, and William Kasper

the party of the second part:

WITNESSETH, That the said party of the first part, for and in consideration of the sum of One and no/100 DOLLARS, lawful money of the United States of America, to them in hand paid by the said party of the second part, the receipt whereof is hereby acknowledged, does by these presents remise, release and convey forever quit-claim unto the said parties of the second part, and to his heirs and assigns, all the certain lot piece or parcel of land situate in the County of Adams, State of Washington, bounded and particularly described as follows, to-wit:

The north half (N½) of the south half (S½) of section ten (10) in township fifteen (15) north, range thirty three (33) E. W. M. containing 160 acres more or less, according the government survey.

TOGETHER with all and singular, the tenements, hereditaments and appurtenances thereunto belonging, or in anywise appertaining, and the reversion and reversions, remainder and remainders, rents, issues and profits thereof.

TO HAVE AND TO HOLD, all and singular, the said premises, together with the appurtenances, unto the said party of the second part, and to his heirs and assigns forever.

IN WITNESS WHEREOF, The parties of the first part have hereunto set our hands and seals the day and year first above written.

Signed, Sealed and Delivered in the presence of

Dan Krehbiel

revenue stamps fifty cents cancelled 8-30-19 J. M.

Johann Nagel (signed in German) (SEAL)

Barbara Nagel (SEAL)

(SEAL)

STATE OF WASHINGTON, County of Adams } ss.

I, Dan Krehbiel, a Notary Public in and for the State of Washington, do hereby certify that on this 30th day of August, A. D. 1919 personally appeared before me, Johann Nagel & Barbara Nagel, his wife to me known to be the individuals described in and who executed the within instrument, and acknowledged that they signed and sealed the same as their free and voluntary act and deed for the uses and purposes therein mentioned.

Given under my hand and official seal, this 30th day of August, A. D. 1919.

SEAL

Dan Krehbiel, Notary Public

Residing at Lind, Washington.

Filed for record Sept. 3, 1919 at 9:7 o'clock A. m., at the request of J. Kasper & Co.

Laura Schrag County Auditor.

Anna Schwerin, Deputy.

Quit Claim Deed, Agreement with Kasper on adjacent land: Sept. 3, 1919 Grantor Nagel, Johann et. ux; Grantee William Kasper; GCH; Recorded Book 53 page 71; Description: N2 S2 of 10 15 33; General Index – Direct, Adams County, Washington, (Selling)

482

QUIT CLAIM DEED

#27894

THIS INDENTURE, Made this 1st day of May, A. D. 1924,

BETWEEN WILLIAM KASPER and HAZEL KASPER, his wife,

the parties of the first part, and JOHN NAGEL,

the party of the second part:

WITNESSETH, That the said parties of the first part, for and in consideration of the sum of ONE DOLLAR and other valuable considerations, - - - - - - - - - - DOLLARS, lawful money of the United States of America, to them in hand paid by the said party of the second part, the receipt whereof is hereby acknowledged, do by these presents remise, release, convey and forever quit claim unto the said party of the second part, and to his heirs and assigns, all that certain real property situate and being in ~~all the real property situate in~~ the County of Adams, and State of Washington, ~~bounded and particularly~~ described as follows, to wit:

The North Half of the South Half of Section Ten (10), Township Fifteen (15) North of Range Thirty-three (33) E.W.M.

TO HAVE AND TO HOLD the said premises,

TOGETHER with all and singular, the tenements, hereditaments and appurtenances thereunto belonging, or in anywise appertaining, and the reversion and reversions, remainder and remainders, rents, issues and profits thereof,

~~TO HAVE AND TO HOLD, all and singular, the said premises, together with the appurtenances,~~ unto the said party of the second part, and to his heirs and assigns forever.

IN WITNESS WHEREOF, The ~~said~~ parties of the first part ha ve hereunto set their hands and seals the day and year first above written.

Executed ~~Signed, sealed and delivered~~ in the presence of

William Kasper (SEAL)

Hazel Kasper (SEAL)

(SEAL)

STATE OF WASHINGTON, ss.

County of Adams

I, C. H. Brittenham, a Notary Public in and for said County and State, ~~the State of Washington~~, do hereby certify that on this 1st day of May, A. D. 1924, personally appeared before me, William Kasper and Hazel Kasper, his wife, to me personally known to be the individuals described in and who executed the within instrument, and acknowledged that they signed ~~and~~ sealed and executed the same as their free and voluntary act and deed for the uses and purposes therein mentioned.

Given under my hand and official seal this 1st day of May, A.D. 1924.

SEAL (Seal)

C. H. Brittenham,
Notary Public ~~in and for the State of Washington~~
Residing at Lind, Wash.

Filed for record June 13, 1924 at 9:32 o'clock A.m., at the request of MacMaster, Ireland

Quit Claim Deed between William Kasper and Hazel Kasper, his wife and John Nagel the North half of the South Half of Section Ten, Township Fifteen North of Range Thirty-three E.W.M. (Section 10, Township 15, Range 33) May 1, 1924. , Book 53 page 482

June 13, 1924 Grantee Nagel, John; Grantor William Kasper et. un; G.C.D; Book 53 page 482; description: N2 S2 of 10 15 33

John extended the mortgage agreement with the bank for the sum of $2,250 with interest until 1928.[35]

Daerheim Transaction

In the county records is also a transaction in September 1924 on a neighboring property with Mike Daerheim which was released the next day. The claim was on the crop of 217 sacks of smutless Turkey Red Wheat harvested in 1924 on the Daerheim property (S23 Tnsp 16 R 33) near John's property and now deposited in a granary on the property. John had been employed at $7.50 a day for operating the combine and $1.00 for each acre harvested with two teams of horses which were $1.75 per day earning $291.25.[36]

The Dormaier family had settled in Quincy from South Dakota and Christ Dormaier had married into the Hockstatter family. Martin is likely related to this family and this would explain the financial transaction as one to a relative.

Martin Dormair is listed in the 1920 US Census for Grant County as age 27 and born in Russia (no Daerheims are listed). He is living with his wife Christina age 27 also born in Russia and two daughters born in S. Dakota – Elsie Ruth age 3 and Laura Alma age 16 months.[37] There is also a Dormaier (Hoefner) Cemetery in Adams County located at T19N R31E Section 19 near the farm but has no marked graves.[38] Martin Dormair died in 1943.[39]

---

[35] Took out Mortgage with US Investment Corp. to cover purchase from Kasper: June 13, 1924 Grantee Nagel, Johannn et. un.; Grantor U.S. Inves. Corp. LD; En. Agrt; Book 66 page 496; N2S2 of 10 15 33; General Index – Reverse, Adams County, Washington, (Buying) a copy is available but not included here.

[36] Took a Claim with Mike Daerheim: Sept 3, 1924 Grantor Nagel, John; Grantee Mike Daerheim; Claim Of Lien; Book 3 page 531; description: Portion of Sec 23 Twp. 16, R 33 lying west of public highway; General Index – Direct, Adams County, Washington, (Selling) a copy is available but not included here.

Release of Claim with Mike Daerheim: Sept 5. 1924 Grantor Nagel, John; Grantee Mike Daerheim; release of Claim Of Lien; Book 3 page 531; General Index – Direct, Adams County, Washington, (Selling) a copy is available but not included here.

[37] GERMAN'S FROM RUSSIA, 1920 U.S. CENSUS, Adams County, Washington Copyright 2001,Eugene Jenkins, 1381 Longmire Lane, Selah, WA 98942 jenkinsgen@nwinfo.net; http://www.webbitt.com/volga/WA-adams-cty.txt

[38] DORMAIER (Hoefner) CEMETERY, Adams County, WA. Transcribed and submitted by Irma Gfeller November 23, 1999. http://files.usgwarchives.net/wa/adams/cemeteries/dormaier.txt

[39] http://wagenweb.org/lincoln/obitsodessavicinitycthrud.htm; Odessa Vicinity Deaths; burial location elsewhere; Submitted by Marge Womach; File 1 Page C through D:**Dormaier:** "Relatives here have been notified of the death of Martin Dormaier, of Olympia, former resident of the Ruff area. His nephew, Adolph Weis, and niece, Mrs Henry Hoefner of Cashmere, left on Monday to attend the funeral." (Odessa Record: 21 Jan 1943)

Mortgages

In January 1928 John took out a mortgage with Kasper and Co. on the property.[40] In November 1928 John paid off the mortgage with the bank[41] but in May took out another mortgage with Kasper & Co.[42] for $26,068 on the 640 total acres (W1/2 of the W1/2 and the SE ¼ of S2; S1/2 of N1/2 and the N1/2 of the S1/2 of Section 10, Township 15 Range 33).

Kasper and Company was the Mercantile in Lind. They would extend credit to the farmers with the deed as collateral (mortgage). Kerry Wahl remembers his grandfather said Barbara liked to spend money at Kasper's store and Jacob Kasper was all too willing to extend credit; "go ahead, we'll put it on your credit." With a bad crop in summer of 1929, John was unable to make payments. The property was transferred to Kasper & Co. in October, 1930.[43]

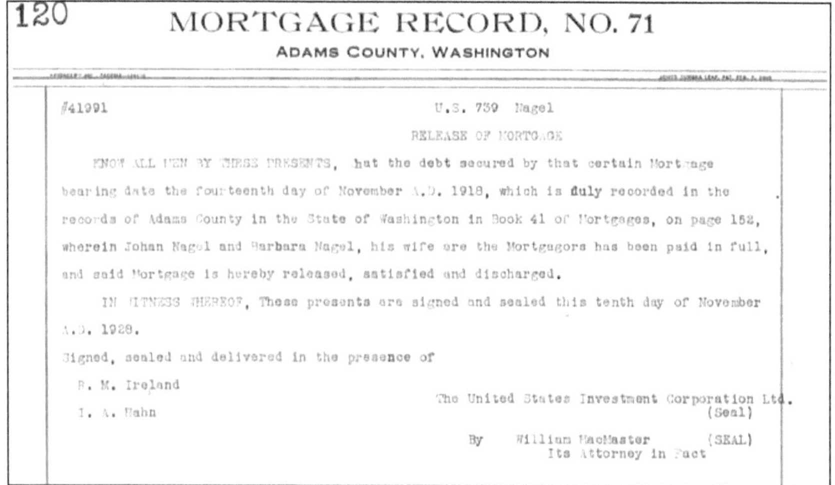

120 MORTGAGE RECORD, NO. 71

ADAMS COUNTY, WASHINGTON

#41991 U.S. 739 Nagel

RELEASE OF MORTGAGE

KNOW ALL MEN BY THESE PRESENTS, that the debt secured by that certain Mortgage bearing date the fourteenth day of November A.D. 1918, which is duly recorded in the records of Adams County in the State of Washington in Book 41 of Mortgages, on page 152, wherein Johan Nagel and Barbara Nagel, his wife are the Mortgagors has been paid in full, and said Mortgage is hereby released, satisfied and discharged.

IN WITNESS WHEREOF, These presents are signed and sealed this tenth day of November A.D. 1928.

Signed, sealed and delivered in the presence of

R. M. Ireland

I. A. Hahn

The United States Investment Corporation Ltd. (Seal)

By William MacMaster (SEAL)
Its Attorney in Fact

Paid back mortgage with US Investment Corp.: Nov. 14 1928 Grantee Nagel, Johann et. ux.; Granter U.S. Investment Corp.; R.M; Book 71 page 120; General Index – Reverse, Adams County, Washington, (Buying)

[40] Took a Mortgage: Jan. 3, 1928 Grantor Nagel, John; Grantee J. Kasper & Co.; Mortgage; Book 69 page 86; General Index – Direct, Adams County, Washington, (Selling)

[41] Paid back mortgage with US Investment Corp.: Nov. 14 1928 Grantee Nagel, Johann et. ux.; Granter U.S. Investment Corp.; R.M; Book 71 page 120; General Index – Reverse, Adams County, Washington, (Buying)

[42] Indenture 1929 Grantor Nagel, John, Grantee J. Kasper & Co. May 28, 1929 for $26,068 on W1/2 of the W1/2 and the SE ¼ of S2; S1/2 of N1/2 and the N1/2 of the S1/2 of Section 10, Township 15 Range 33 containing 640 acres.

[43] Transferred to Kasper: *Oct 2, 1929 (date from index, actual date on deed is October, 1930) Grantor Nagel, Johann; Grantee William Kasper – Trustee; Warranty Deed; Book 64 page 123; General Index – Direct, Adams County, Washington, (Selling) See document.

[Mtg. 69/149]

43372

This Indenture, made this 28th day of May, A. D. 1929 between John Nagel and Barbara Nagel, his wife the parties of the first part, and J. Kasper & Co., a co-partnership consisting of Jacob Kasper and William Kasper the parties of the second part,

Witnesseth, That the said parties of the first part, for and in consideration of the sum of Twenty-six Thousand Sixty-eight and 89/100 ($26,068.89) Dollars, lawful money of the United States, to them in hand paid by the said parties of the second part, the receipt whereof is hereby acknowledged, do by these presents grant, bargain, sell, convey and confirm unto the said parties of the second part, and to their heirs and assigns, the following described tract or parcel of land, lying and being in the County of Adams, and State of Washington, to-wit:

Lot Four (4); Southwest Quarter (SW¼) of the Northwest Quarter (NW¼); West Half (W½) of the Southwest Quarter (SW¼) also described as the West Half (W½) of the West Half (W½) and the Southeast Quarter (SE¼) of Section Two (2); South Half (S½) of the North half (N½) and the North Half (N½) of the South Half (S½) of Section Ten (10) Township Fifteen (15) North, Range Thirty-three (33) E.W.M. containing six hundred forty acres more or less according to the government survey thereof.

Together with all and singular the tenements, hereditaments and appurtenances thereunto belonging:

This conveyance is intended as a Mortgage to secure the payment of Twenty-six Thousand Sixty-eight and 89/100 ($26,068.89) Dollars, lawful money of the United States, together with interest thereon in like lawful money at the rate of 10 per cent. per annum from date until paid, according to the terms and conditions of one certain promissory note bearing date Jan. 21, 1929 made by John Nagel and Barbara Nagel, his wife payable Sept. 1, 1929 to the order of J. Kasper & Co., a co-partnership consisting of Jacob Kasper and William Kasper and these presents shall be void if such payment be made according to the terms and conditions thereof. But in case default be made in the payment of the principal or interest of said promissory note, or any part thereof, when the same shall become due and payable, according to the terms and conditions thereof, then the said parties of the second part, their executors, administrators and assigns may foreclose this mortgage and the said premises, with all and every of the appurtenances, or any part thereof, in the manner prescribd by law, and out of the money arising from such sale, retain the whole of said principal and interest, whether the same shall be then due or not, together with the costs and charges of making such sale, and the overplus, if any there be, shall be paid by the parties making such sale, on demand, to the said parties of the first part, their heirs or assigns. And in any suit or other proceedings that may be had for the recovery of said principal sum and interest on either said note or this mortgage, it shall and may be lawful for the said parties of the second part, their heirs, executors, administrators or assigns, to include in the judgment that may be recovered, a reasonable sum for attorney's fees in such case, or in case of settlement or payment being made after suit has been commenced, and before the final decree has been entered thereon, an attorney's fee of Dollars, in lawful money, shall be taxed as part of the costs in such suit—as well as all payments that the said parties of the second part, their heirs, executors, administrators or assigns may be obliged to make for its or their security by insurance or on account of any taxes, charges, incumbrances, or assessments whatsoever on the said premises or any part thereof.

In Testimony Whereof, the said parties of the first part have hereunto set their hands and seals the day and year first above written.

Executed in the presence of

John Nagel (Signed in German) (Seal)
Barbara Nagel (Seal)
(Seal)
(Seal)

STATE OF WASHINGTON,
County of Adams } ss.

I, C. H. Brittenham a Notary Public in and for said County and State do hereby certify that on this 6th day of June, A. D. 1929, personally appeared before me John Nagel and Barbara Nagel, his wife to me known to be the individuals described in and who executed the within instrument, and acknowledged that they signed and executed the same as their free and voluntary act and deed, for the uses and purposes therein mentioned.

Given under my hand and official seal this 6th day of June, A. D. 1929.

(Seal)

C. H. Brittenham
Notary Public, Residing at Lind, Washington.

RELEASED Feb 7 1936 LENA BUHL, County Auditor By [illegible] Deputy

Filed for record June 13 A. D. 1929, at 9:02 A.M.
Laura Schragg
Auditor.
Recorded by Mabel Bierman
Mabel Bierman
Deputy.

Indenture 1929 Grantor Nagel, John, Grantee J. Kasper & Co. May 28, 1929 for $26,068 on W1/2 of the W1/2 and the SE ¼ of S2; S1/2 of N1/2 and the N1/2 of the S1/2 of Section 10, Township 15 Range 33 containing 640 acres

WARRANTY DEED

No. 46979

John Nagel

TO

J. Kasper & Co.

STATE OF WASHINGTON, Adams County—ss.
Filed for Record the 2 day of Oct., 19 30, at 8 o'clock and 40 minutes A. M., at request of J. Kasper & Company

Laura Schragg
County Auditor.

By Mabel Bierman
Deputy.

Recorded by Mabel Bierman
Deputy.

THIS INDENTURE, Made this 1st day of October A. D. 1930, between Johann Nagel, sometimes signed Johan Nagel and sometimes John Nagel, and Barbara Nagel, his wife part ies of the first part, and William Kasper, trustee for J. Kasper & Company a co-partnership consisting of Jacob Kasper and William Kasper parties of the second part,

WITNESSETH, That the said part ies of the first part, for and in consideration of the sum of Twenty-two Thousand Four Hundred and no/100 ($22,400.00) DOLLARS, to them in hand paid by the said parties of the second part, the receipt whereof is hereby acknowledged, do hereby grant, bargain, sell, convey and confirm unto the said parties of the second part, their heirs and assigns forever, that certain real property situate and being in the County of Adams, State of Washington, and described as follows, to-wit:

West Half of the West Half (W½ W½) and the Southeast Quarter (SE¼) of Section Two (2); South Half of the North Half (S½ N½) and the North Half of the South Half (N½ S½) of Section Ten (10) all in Township Fifteen (15) North, Range Thirty-three (33) E.W.M.

TO HAVE AND TO HOLD THE SAME, Together with all the hereditaments and appurtenances thereunto belonging or in any wise appertaining to the said parties of the second part their heirs and assigns forever. And the said Johann Nagel and Barbara Nagel, his wife parties of the first part, for themselves and their heirs, executors and administrators, do covenant with the said parties of the second part, their heirs and assigns, that they are well seized in fee of the lands and premises aforesaid, and have good right to sell and convey the same in manner and form aforesaid; that the same are free from all incumbrances; except the last half of 1929 taxes.

and the above bargained and granted lands and premises, in the quiet and peaceable possession of the said parties of the second part, their heirs and assigns, against all persons lawfully claiming, or to claim, the whole or any part thereof, the said parties of the first part will warrant and forever defend.

IN TESTIMONY WHEREOF, The said parties of the first part have hereunto set their hands and seals the day and year first above written.

Executed in Presence of

Johann Nagel (Signed in German) (SEAL)
Barbara Nagel (SEAL)
(SEAL)
(SEAL)

STATE OF WASHINGTON, County of Adams } ss.

I, C. H. Brittenham a Notary Public in and for the State of Washington do hereby certify that on this 1st day of October A. D. 1930, personally appeared before me Johann Nagel and Barbara Nagel his wife to me known to be the individuals described in and who executed the within instrument, and acknowledged that they signed and sealed the same as their free and voluntary act and deed for the uses and purposes therein mentioned.

Given under my hand and official seal this 1st day of October A.D. 1930.

C. H. Brittenham

Warranty Deed between John Nagel and J. Kasper & Co., dated October 2, 1930 for West Half of the West Half and the Southeast Quarter of Section Two; South Half of North Half and the North Half of the South Half of Section Ten all in Township Fifteen North, Range Thirty-three E.W.M. (Section 10, Township 15, Range 33) Book 64 page 123
In consideration for the sum of $22,400

William Kasper, trustee for J. Kasper & Company a co-partnership consisting of Jacob Kasper and William Kasper. Johann Nagel and Barbara Nagel, his wife; Johann Hagel (signed in German) Oct 2, 1929 (wrong date entered in Index book) Grantor Nagel, Johann; Grantee William Kasper – Trustee; Warranty Deed; Book 64 page 123

In family stories John took the best horses to Barbara's sister (aunt Lydia) to hide from the creditors. There is a Lydia Huether age 21 listed in Grant County Census living with Barbara's family.[44]

There is a Lydia Huether (age 20) living in Spokane County Plaza Township with her brother Chris age 35 and wife Elizabeth age 32 and their family Reinhold age 10, Leo age 9, Elizabeth age 3, Frieta age 2 and Herman one month old.[45]

Also nearby between Lind and Paha in the 1920's was Barbara Ottmar Borth who was related through the Ottmars.[46]

---

[44] 1920 U.S. CENSUS, Grant County, Washington; Copyright 2001,Eugene Jenkins, 1381 Longmire Lane, Selah, WA 98942; jenkinsgen@nwinfo.net, http://www.webbitt.com/volga/WA-grant-cty.txt

[45] 1920 U.S. CENSUS, Spokane County, Washington; Copyright 2001,Eugene Jenkins, 1381 Longmire Lane, Selah, WA 98942; jenkinsgen@nwinfo.net, http://www.webbitt.com/volga/WA-spokane-cty.txt; she may have been double counted?

[46] **Borth, Barbara: (b. Apr 09, 1901, d. May 02, 1964)** Barbara Ottmar Borth, born April 9, 1901 in Russia, the daughter of the Jacob Ottmars, came to America as an infant where the family resided at Ruff. She married Rudolph Borth Dec 19, 1922 and they resided near Lind and Paha. She died at the age of 63, burial in the Lind Cemetery. She is survived by her husband and 5 children: Mrs. George (Eleanor) Pence of Lind; Mrs. Reinhold (Gloria) Sackmann of Lind; and Mrs. Donald (Barbara) Van Buren of Lewiston, ID; Victor, of Lind; and Cleve of East Wenatchee; her mother, Mrs. Jacob Ottmar of Odessa; two sisters: Mrs. Jake Schmauder of Davenport; Mrs. Archie Zickler of Marlin; six brothers: John and Jake Ottmar of Coulee City; Bill Ottmar of Brewster; Ben Ottmar of Davenport; Rynold Ottmar of Spokane. (notes from Odessa Record: 5-14-1964)
http://wagenweb.org/lincoln/obitslindcemathrul.htm

The Property Today

The property is owned by Kerry Wahl.

John purchased the land from James Neilson in November of 1917. This was the North half of Southeast quarter and North Half of the Southwest quarter of Section 10 Township 15 Range 33. (T15R33S10)

In 1919 John made an agreement with Jacob Kasper to purchase on the adjacent land (North half South half of T15R33S10) which he paid off in 1924.

In January 1928 John took out a mortgage with Kasper and Co. on the property. In November 1928 John paid off the mortgage with the bank but in May took out a mortgage with Kasper & Co. for $26,068 on the 640 total acres (W1/2 of the W1/2 and the SE ¼ of S2; S1/2 of N1/2 and the N1/2 of the S1/2 of Section 10, Township 15 Range 33).

With a bad crop in summer of 1929, John was unable to make payments. The property was transferred to Kasper & Co. in October, 1930.

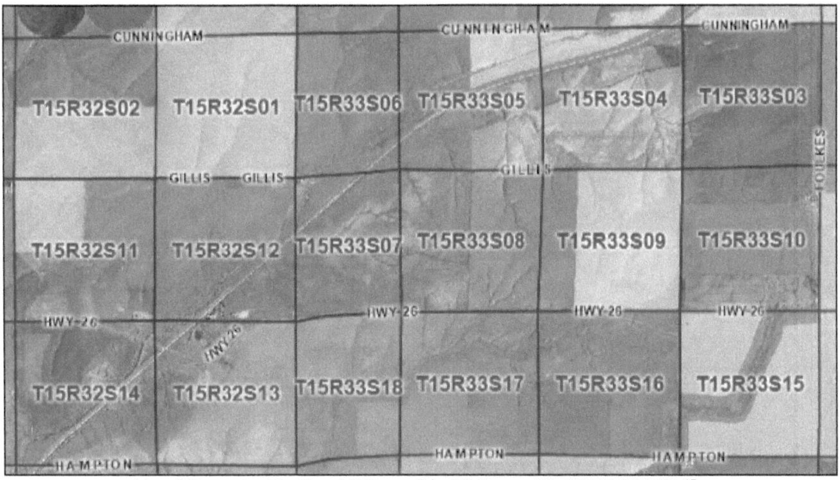

Nagel Property, Section 10 Township 15 Range 33. (T15R33S10) [47]

[47] http://adamswa.mapsifter.com/default.aspx

Nagel Property, Section 10 Township 15 Range 33. (T15R33S10)[48]

[48] http://adamswa.mapsifter.com/default.aspx

Nagel Property, Close up of house and barns.
Section 10 Township 15 Range 33. (T15R33S10)[49]

[49] http://adamswa.mapsifter.com/default.aspx

ADAMS COUNTY ASSESSOR'S OFFICE

Real Property Record Card — TerraSca

Data Provided By: SHERRI L BREWER County Assessor. Printed on 08/12/2011 at 02:40:55P

Parcel Information		Ownership Information	
Parcel Number	2533100100001	Current Owner	WAHL, KERRY DUANE
Map Number	1533-10-10-000000-000-00020		
Situs	FOULKES & HWY 26	Address	724 S FOULKES RD
Legal	S1/2N1/2 & N1/2S1/2 SEC 10, TWP 15, RGE 33 LESS TAX #1074 & RD	City ST. Zip	LIND, WA 99341-

Market Value		Assessed Value		Property Classification	
Impr Value		Impr Value		District	39
Land Value	139,500	Land Value	74,400	Neighborhood	13
Perm Crop Value		Perm Crop Value		Class Code	83 00 00
Total Value	139,500	Total Value	74,400	Ex Code	
Open Space	Yes	Frozen Value		Exemption	
OSP Date	05/01/1998	Taxable Value	74,400	Dd Acres	310.05

Miscellaneous Assessment Data

Miscellaneous Assessments		Acre Totals		Acre Totals	
GWMA Dist		Dry Acres	310.050	Timber Acres	
Weed Control	166	Irrg Acres		Total Acres	310.050
Pest Control		Other Acres		PC Acres	
Pest Control Acres		Site Acres		DNR Acres	

Sales History — Multiple Owner Information

Adams County Assessor's Office Real Property Record; 310 Acres

ADAMS COUNTY ASSESSOR'S OFFICE

Real Property Record Card — TerraS

Data Provided By: SHERRI L BREWER County Assessor. Printed on 08/12/2011 at 02:42:17P

Parcel Information		Ownership Information	
Parcel Number	2533100141074	Current Owner	WAHL, KERRY
Map Number	1533-10-14-000000-000-00000		
Situs	724 S FOULKES RD	Address	724 S FOULKES RD
Legal	TAX #1074 IN NE1/4 SEC 10, TWP 15, RGE 33 DESCRIBED AS FOLLOWS:	City ST. Zip	LIND, WA 99341-0000

Market Value		Assessed Value		Property Classification	
Impr Value	122,700	Impr Value	122,700	District	39
Land Value	17,600	Land Value	2,200	Neighborhood	13
Perm Crop Value		Perm Crop Value		Class Code	83 00 00
Total Value	140,300	Total Value	124,900	Ex Code	
Open Space	Yes	Frozen Value		Exemption	
OSP Date	05/01/1998	Taxable Value	124,900	Dd Acres	8.95

Miscellaneous Assessment Data

Miscellaneous Assessments		Acre Totals		Acre Totals	
GWMA Dist		Dry Acres	7.950	Timber Acres	
Weed Control	166	Irrg Acres		Total Acres	8.950
Pest Control		Other Acres		PC Acres	
Pest Control Acres		Site Acres	1.000	DNR Acres	

Sales History — Multiple Owner Information

Date | Book/Page | Grantor | Price | Ownrshp % | Owner's Name

Adams County Assessor's Office Real Property Record: 8.9 acres with house

ADAMS COUNTY ASSESSOR'S OFFICE

Real Property Record Card — TerraS

Data Provided By: SHERRI L BREWER County Assessor. Printed on 08/12/2011 at 02:44:17P

Parcel Information		Ownership Information	
Parcel Number	2533100200001	Current Owner	WAHL, KERRY
Map Number	1533-10-10-000000-000-00010		
Situs		Address	724 S FOULKES RD
Legal	N1/2N1/2 SEC 10, TWP 15, RGE 33 LESS A PTN OF TAX #1074 & RD	City ST. Zip	LIND, WA 99341-0000

Market Value		Assessed Value		Property Classification	
Impr Value		Impr Value		District	39
Land Value	70,400	Land Value	37,500	Neighborhood	13
Perm Crop Value		Perm Crop Value		Class Code	83 00 00
Total Value	70,400	Total Value	37,500	Ex Code	
Open Space	Yes	Frozen Value		Exemption	
OSP Date	05/01/1998	Taxable Value	37,500	Dd Acres	157.00

Miscellaneous Assessment Data

Miscellaneous Assessments		Acre Totals		Acre Totals	
GWMA Dist		Dry Acres	157.000	Timber Acres	
Weed Control	166	Irrg Acres		Total Acres	157.000
Pest Control		Other Acres		PC Acres	
Pest Control Acres		Site Acres		DNR Acres	

Sales History — Multiple Owner Information

Date | Book/Page | Grantor | Price | Ownrshp % | Owner's Name

Adams County Assessor's Office Real Property Record: 157 acres

Directions to the property

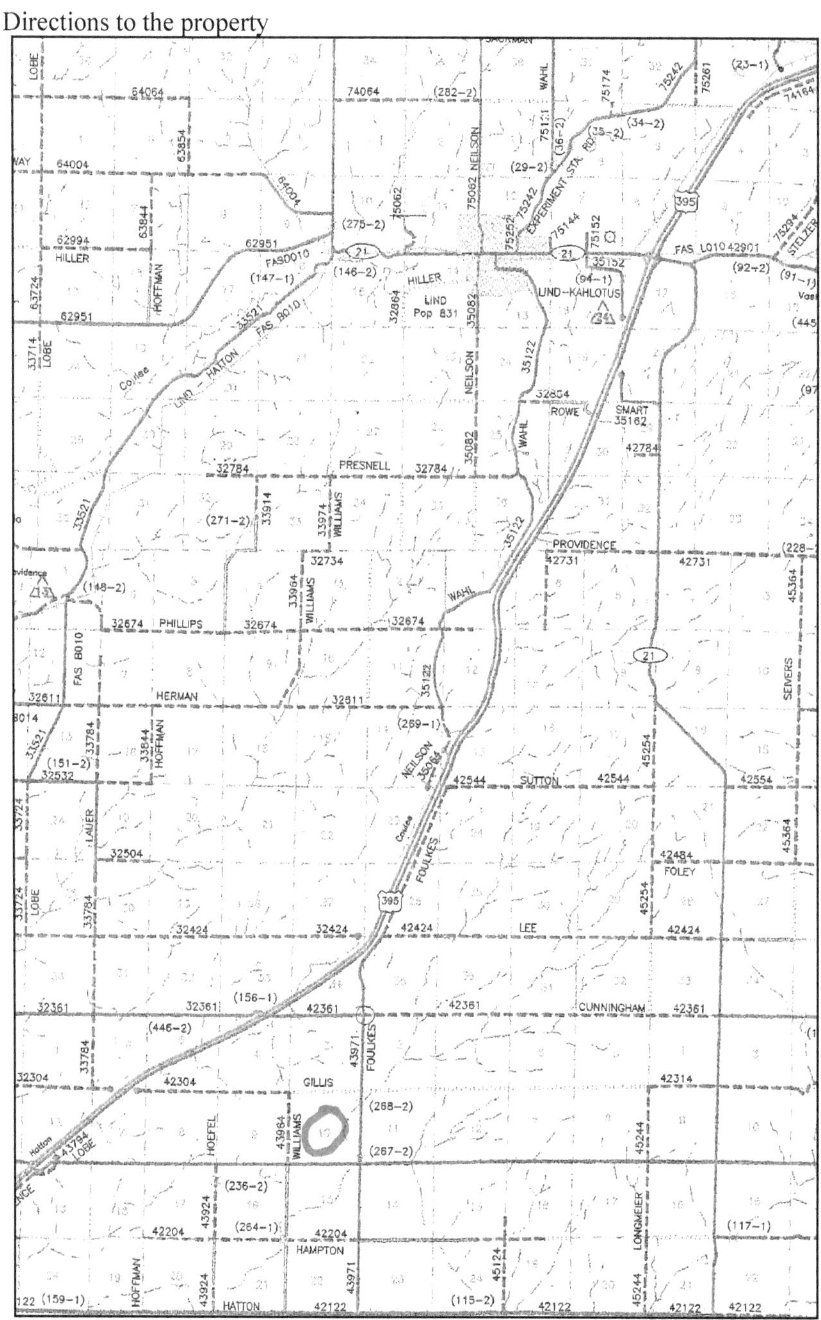

Going south on US-395 from I90 heading to Pasco go 25 miles and turn left onto Cunningham Road. Go 1.2 miles and turn right onto Foulkes Road; 724 Foulkes Road is on the right before you get to WA-26. It is about 30 minutes from Ritzville and about 12 miles south of Lind. If you miss the left onto Cunningham Road you can take a right onto WA-26 turning left and travel down WA-26 to Foulkes Road and take a right.

724 S Foulkes Road, Lind WA 99341-9731

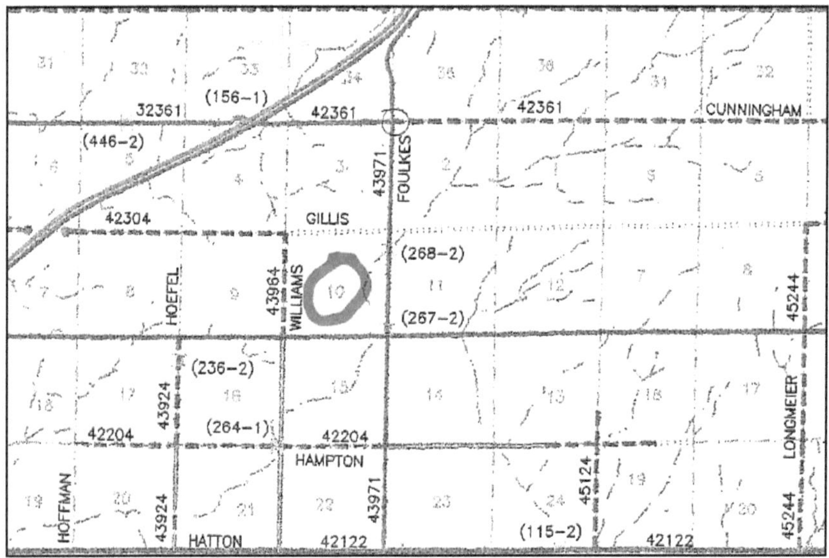

Foulkes Road and Cunningham Road, Old Nagel farm in Lind,
724 S Foulkes Road, Lind WA

From the north, Old Nagel farm in Lind, 724 S Foulkes Road, Lind WA

From the north, Old Nagel farm in Lind, 724 S Foulkes Road, Lind WA

Foulkes Road turn from Highway 26,
if you miss the Cunningham turn you can come upon the farm from the south

Street view of Old Nagel farm in Lind, 724 S Foulkes Road, Lind WA

Front of old farm house, Old Nagel farm in Lind, 724 S Foulkes Road, Lind WA

South Side old farm house, Old Nagel farm in Lind, 724 S Foulkes Road, Lind WA

David standing in front of old Nagel farm in Lind, 724 S Foulkes Road, Lind WA

Back of house from the north, Old Nagel farm in Lind, 724 S Foulkes Road, Lind WA

Big barn, Old Nagel farm in Lind, 724 S Foulkes Road, Lind WA

Interior of big barn, Old Nagel farm in Lind, 724 S Foulkes Road, Lind WA

Old equipment outside Old Nagel farm in Lind, 724 S Foulkes Road, Lind WA

North barn, Old Nagel farm in Lind, 724 S Foulkes Road, Lind WA

House from the north, Old Nagel farm in Lind, 724 S Foulkes Road, Lind WA

Directions to Lind

Turn off of I90 to Lind, Washington, taken September 2010

Heading south to Lind, Washington, taken September 2010

Coming into Lind, Washington, taken September 2010

Lind, Washington looking north, taken September 2010

Lind, Washington looking west, taken September 2010

Cunningham

Cunningham was a small town with a railroad depot about 12 miles south of Lind. Cunningham is the nearest town to the Nagel farm but it no longer exists. The farm has always been referred to as near Lind.

Cunningham pictures from Adams County Historical Society

03-00153 cunningham.tif

03-00150 cunningham.tif

03-01956 cunningham school.tif

03-01496 cunningham residential street.tif

Kasper's

Kasper & Company was the local mercantile in Lind and the company that took the Nagel farm.

Lind Washington, One story brick, center left is the Kasper Mercantile

Transcribed from "An Illustrated History of The Big Bend Country, embracing Lincoln, Douglas, Adams and Franklin counties, State of Washington", published by Western Historical Publishing Co., 1904.

> JACOB KASPER is handling the largest general store in Lind, where he has been established for some years. He is a merchant of wide experience and his success here has demonstrated his ability to be of a high order. His establishment is located on the main street of the town and is a one-story brick, which is entirely occupied with his merchandise. The basement is utilized for storing goods and the stock carried here is worth more than fifty-five thousand dollars. Mr. Kasper has shown marked wisdom in selecting his goods for he has a fine variety of all kinds adapted to this trade, and the motto, "Well bought, half sold" is one which he heeds well, for he is a careful and shrewd buyer knows how to get bargains for his customers. This has drawn a very large patronage to his store, which his careful business methods have held.
>
> Jacob Kasper was born in Poland, on January 7, 1855, the son of Jacob and Sarah Kasper. His boyhood days were spent in his native country and there he was favored with a good educational training. When he had arrived at his majority, he determined to try the larger and more inviting fields of the new world and accordingly came hither ready for business. He located in San Francisco and there secured employment as salesman in a general store. He made the most of his

opportunities and soon was well acquainted with the lines of business here and had made good headway in mastering the English language. Then he started a store for himself. This was eighteen months after he landed. Soon he removed to Forest Hill, California, and conducted a mercantile establishment there for two years. His next location was in Walla Walla, where he opened a dry goods store in company with W. Rudee. He soon bought out his partner and continued the store until 1890. Then he removed to Farmington, Washington, and there conducted a general store until 1893. On account of the panic that then swept the country he lost heavily. After that, he opened business in Kendrick, Idaho, the largest store in the town, and did business there until 1901. In that year he and his brother opened a wholesale woodenware and basket house in San Francisco, under the firm name of Kasper Brothers & Company. Leaving the management of the concern to his brother he came to Lind and started the business which has grown to the present large dimensions under his supervision. The business has the form of a large department store and would do credit to a city, and Lind is to be congratulated that Mr. Kasper has been induced to make this his headquarters. The building utilized is owned by Mr. Kasper and is fifty by one hundred feet. It is packed from roof to basement floor with the choicest goods and is the center of great activity. In 1904 Mr. Kasper sold his San Francisco venture and is giving his entire attention to the management and building up of his Lind store. Believing that the country will justify it, he has led in the mercantile business in his town, and determines to make his the best store in the county in due time.

Mr. Kasper is a strong Republican and takes a keen interest in every movement, both political and educational, as he is very progressive and public minded. He is a member of the I. O. O. F. and is a leading citizen of Lind.

At San Francisco, on April 27, 1890, Mr. Kasper married Miss Esther Lewis, a native of Poland. She came to this country with her parents when six years of age and lived in San Francisco, where she was reared and educated. Her parents died in that city. To Mr. and Mrs. Kasper, one child has been born, Sylven L., aged thirteen.

Jacob Kasper's obituary ran in the Ritzville Journal-Times, Thursday, April 6, 1933.[50]

Death Calls Jacob Kasper

LIND - Jacob Kasper, a resident of the northwest and of Lind for about 35 years, passed away at his home in Lind Sunday noon, April 2. The Smith funeral home of Spokane had charge of the funeral arrangements. The deceased leaves his aged wife and a son, Slyvan, of San Francisco, who was here for the funeral.

J. Kasper & company, of which Mr. Kasper was the head, operated for a long number of years the largest department and general store in the western part of the county. This firm also became interested in a large acreage of land and in former years Mr. Kasper was of much benefit throughout the entire district for the help extended to a large number of people.

Mr. Kasper was a member of the Temple Emanuel of San Francisco, Calif. I.O.O.F. Harmony No. 13 and B'nai of Spokane.

[50] Ritzville Journal-Times, Thursday, April 6, 1933, issue http://files.usgwarchives.net/wa/adams/obits/1933-2.txt

Location of Kasper General Mercantile in Lind Washington;
it burned down and was replaced by this trailer.

Move to Spangle

Dorothy, Edna, Anna, Gertie, Herby, Harold (behind Herby), and Bud Kauth (holding rabbit)
Spangle, Washington, 20 miles south of Spokane,
About 1934 – 1935

The family moved to Spangle in about 1932. Spangle is about fifteen or twenty miles south of Spokane. Herby was a baby. About the time they got there, the eight or ten cows were all dry. The neighbors would give the family milk. One day mama's relatives visited, a brother and family. Harold drank pickle brine and almost died. Herding cows in Spangle, the cows needed to be moved up the road about two or three miles to another farm. Edna and Anna took the cows up once and heard coyotes howling. The howling scared them both and they took the cows home early. The neighbors had one bull and the family another. The kids were in new jeans. Taking the cows up once, the two bulls started fighting. Anna made a run for the fence to crawl under and ripped her new pants.

The kids where always told to stay out (Spangle) of papa's wooden chest. Once Charlie and Johnnie picked the lock to the chest and got the pistol. The family in the living room heard the gun go off. It almost killed Charlie, with Johnnie holding the gun.

In Spangle, Edna would go get the cows and would sing Jesus Loves Me at the top of her voice. A little grandma named Miller heard her and gave her a doll. The doll is now 125 years old.

In Spangle, when Edna was 8 or 9 years old, they had a walnut tree out in the orchard. The kids took the 6 foot ladder from the windmill and placed it on a barrel to pick walnuts. It collapsed and Edna fell and knocked herself out. It scarred Anna. Anna was the one who said "get us some walnuts".

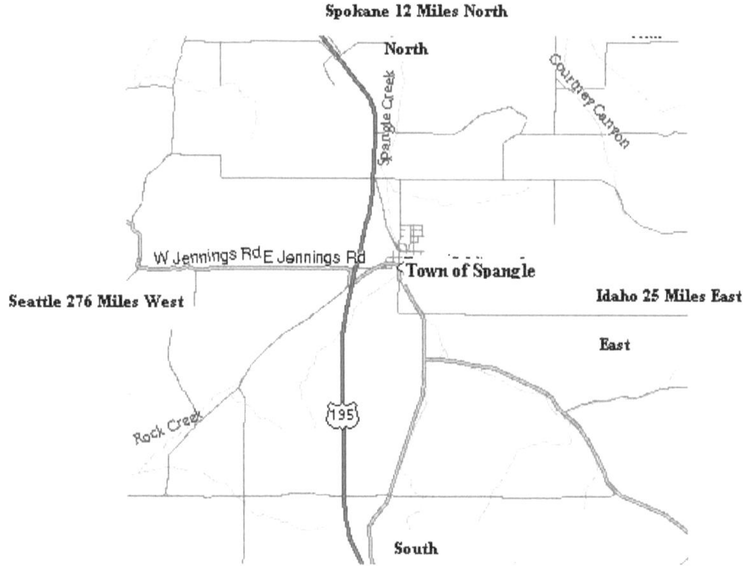

Historic Spangle (founded 1872) is located 12 miles south of Spokane on Highway 195.

Spangle from the Highway looking Southeast, taken September 2010

Spangle welcome sign

Main Street Spangle, looking north

The school at Spangle, no longer in use

Spangle from the South looking North

Anna places the farm north of town. She said nothing is standing, not even the windmill.

Newman Lake

Harold and Herby
Harold about 7 or 8, at Newman Lake, Barn, granary and bunk house is to right About 1938-39, The timber in the back is where they turned the cows loose, they would ride horses up to get the cows. About 13 miles from Rathdrum.

The Nagel family moved to Newman Lake about 1935. They had rented in Spangle and they rented at Newman Lake too. Edna was in the sixth grade in a one-room schoolhouse with one teacher up to the sixth grade. The house was up a draw. There is a housing division there now. The man who owned the property had a little puppy named Feller. The couple was old and the puppy would come down and play with the kids. He was collie like. Once, Edna was walking down the road with him and Feller would get in her way and not let her pass. Edna saw up the road a big bull snake. The puppy had been protecting her.

Dorothy got pneumonia at Newman Lake and was taken to the Deaconess Spokane hospital by the landlord who lived up the hill.

There was a little horse that had a colt that was very small. It was too small to be a workhorse. The kids called him the Burrow and made papa let the family keep him. It was about the size of a Shetland pony. Once up in the field, the coyotes ran a bunch of the horses into a fence. Several horses, including Burrow were cut across the chest by the fence and had to be shot.

They had a horse named Alic. He was brought up from Lind. The horse was getting old. Papa wanted Charlie to take him up on the ridge and shoot him and place traps around. Charlie came back about an hour later leading Alic. He couldn't shoot him.

The kids would walk to and from school across the alfalfa field. Once on the way home, the cows had gotten though the fence and into the wet alfalfa. Edna saw four or five cows die of bloat with nothing that could be done.

Once after papa had sold the wheat, the family went into town to buy school clothes. Edna remembers Anna saying to her "stay in the lines" as they walked across the streets. Edna never saw any lines and was confused.

On Edna's eleventh birthday at Newman Lake, Edna was feeling so gown up. Anna said she was just eleven and Edna cried again.

Once, mama and papa had a terrible argument. Papa got the gun out and was going to fix mama, and threatened to shoot the whole family. Anna and Edna hid in the cellar. They always fought, maybe having eight kids through the depression was too much. Mama always said she wanted a divorce and was always saying to the kids, "who do you want to go with papa or me?"

Papa only shaved on Sunday morning. Edna would sit with her elbows on the table and watch him. He would puff out his cheeks. Edna has his shaving mug that he brought from Russia. The handle is broken, but has always been.

Edna remembers returning to Newman Lake and visiting the farm and seeing missile silos in the old alfalfa field.

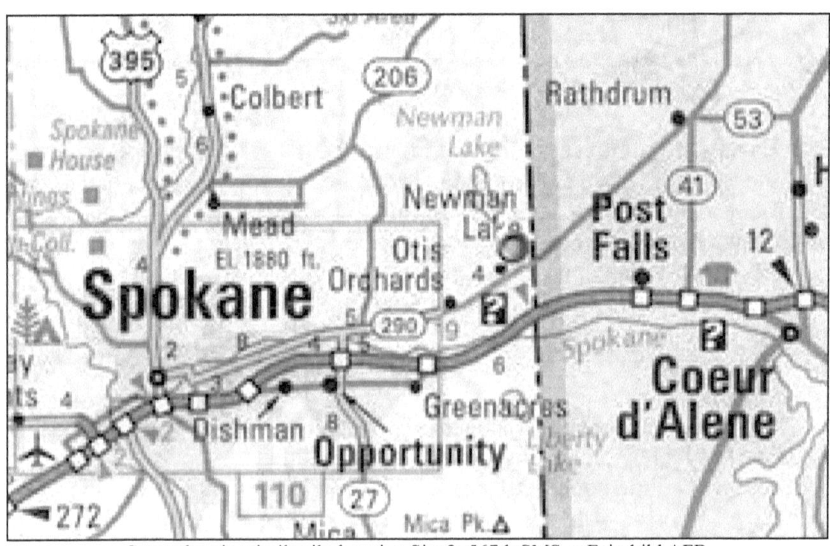

Green dote is missile silo location Site 2, 567th SMS at Fairchild AFB

There were nine Atlas E complexes which were assigned to the 567th SMS at Fairchild AFB in Spokane, Washington.

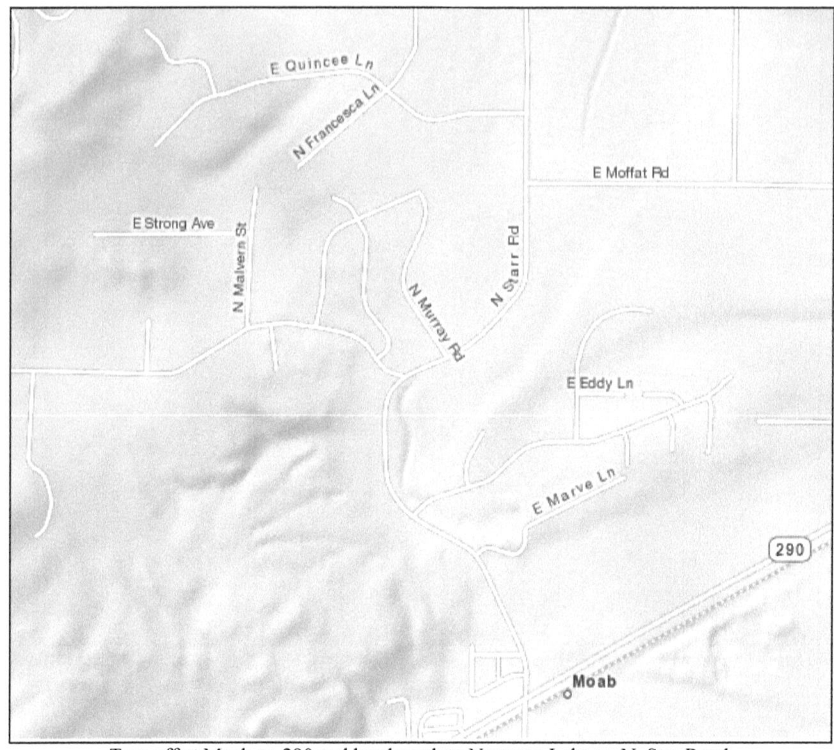

Turn off at Moab on 290 and head north to Newman Lake on N. Star Road

You can get to an overlooking ridge by turning from N. Star (the Newman Lake Road) left (west) onto E. Morris Rd. Then right on N Malvern St. and then left (west) on E. Strong Ave. and going to the end of the road or just following Malvern St.

There is also a nice drive by turning on left W. Newman Lake Dr. and then go straight at the turn onto E. Winter Pine Ln. heading east. This heads up the ridge and turns into N Elk Ln. This area overlooks the farm.

Close up of old farm property and missile silo

Looking west from the housing division, Newman Lake farm, September 2010

Looking south from Carver U-Pick farm towards the Newman Lake farm

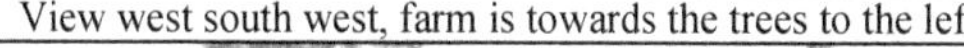
View west south west, farm is towards the trees to the left

Looking south at the missile silo through the trees

Looking north east from about the farm at Newman Lake

View east from the upper farm at Newman Lake

Missile silo gate (now privately owned)

Close up of gate

Rathdrum

In 1939 or 1940 or 41, the Nagel's moved to Rathdrum.

When Edna moved to Rathdrum, she was a junior in High School. It was just a mile out of town to the south. Edna met a guy named Les Jordan, a friend of Charlie when Edna was about 15. They started dating, and when the war started they got engaged. Edna was in the senior play. There were only 26 in the class. "There's a gal that has too much on the ball to stay in town". Edna broke it off with a "Dear John" letter, she didn't want to be married to a stump farmer. He was going to send her the money to come to Florida where he was stationed. He was married two or three years later.

Charlie always said that I don't want to own the whole prairie; I just want to own the land that adjoins mine.

Historical sign outside Rathdrum

John and Barbara Nagel, about 1960

Bobby,?, Johnny?; 3rd over Anna Harms, 4th Augie Harms, 6th over Gertie, in back Walter Lindstrom,
At the end, John Nagel, Front, Peeking out is Barbara Ann
In front of Gertie is Bea? About 1955 – 56
Rick and Steve in front?

Edna, Dorothy, Barbara (mother) and Anna Harms (Nagel, married Johnnie Nagel)
On the farm one mile out of Rathdrum, (Johnnie in truck,)
Granary in background, 1942-43

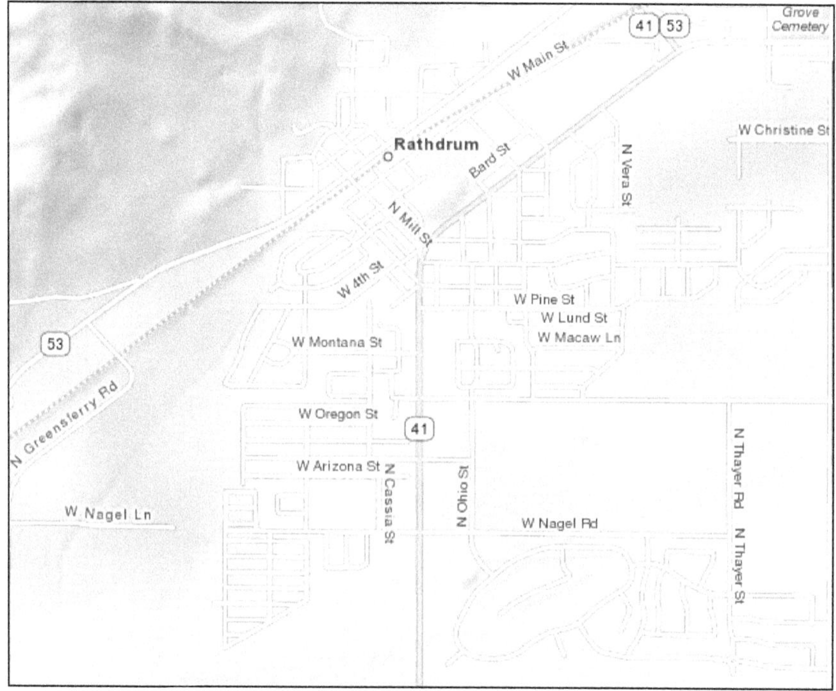

Rathdrum, note W. Nagel Lane and W. Nagel Rd

Area of the farm, Nagel Lane and Nagel Street near bottom
The Willow Creek Mobile Home Park is near the top right,
Anna's house is right at Highway 53 and Hidden Valley road

Rathdrum Welcome sign, taken September 2010

Field south of town was Nagel property

Nagel Street sign on the south side of town

Willow Creek Mobile Home Park built on Nagel property

This was the old drug store where Ed and David bought Cherry Sodas

The High School that Edna went to, taken 2010

Grandma and Grandpa rented this house in town and that is where we visited them when I was growing up, taken 2010

The Church across from Grandma's house

Pinegrove Cemetery, Rathdrum, Kootenai County, ID

Many of the family are buried in the family plot at Pinegrove Cemetery in Rathdrum. The Pinegrove Cemetery is located just east of the town of Rathdrum on Highway 53.

Nagel, Anna Laura 1922 12-23-1960 s/s John Jr.
Nagel, Barbara 08-23-1895 07-03-1994 s/s John Sr.
Nagel, Carl 07-11-1919 11-05-1991
Nagel, Claude Joe 03-07-1948 05-12-1948 s/p Ernie C
Nagel, Ernie Carl 09-23-1945 01-20-1980 s/p Claude J
Nagel, John Jr. 01-25-1918 05-21-1975 s/s Anna L
Nagel, John Sr. 1883 04-20-1962 s/s Barbara

S/P SAME PLOT
S/S SAME STONE

Directions to the cemetery are: take Highway 41 north from I90 to the town of Rathdrum. At the Highway 41and Highway 53 interchange go straight so that you stay on Highway 53. Go around the corner and you will see a Super One Foods Store on your right. The cemetery is just east of this location on the North side of the road. The entrance is off Highway 53. This is one of the oldest cemeteries in either Kootenai or Bonner County. Rathdrum was the original county seat for Kootenai County. Until approximately 1910 Bonner County was part of Kootenai County.

Pine Grove cemetery gate

NAGEL, Anna Laura 1922 - Dec. 23, 1960 .... Block 37 #4
NAGEL, Barbara 1895 - July 3, 1994 .... Block 37 #4
NAGEL, Carl Jul. 11, 1919 - Nov. 5, 1991 .... Block 31 #12
NAGEL, Carl "Ernie" Sept. 23, 1945 - Jan. 20, 1980 .... Block 31 #12
NAGEL, Claude Joe Mar. 7, 1948 - May 12, 1948 .... Block 31 #12
NAGEL, Harold Apr. 9, 1927 - Feb. 25, 2005 (cremains between Mom & Dad) .... Block 37 #4
NAGEL, John Sr. 1883 - Apr. 20, 1962 .... Block 37 #4
NAGEL, John Jr. Jan. 25, 1918 - May 21, 1975 .... Block 37 #4
NAGEL, Violet Mar. 5, 1926 – Jan. 20, 2008 .... Block 31 #12
NAPIER, Elijah A. 1879 - 1953 .... Block 34 #6
NAPIER, Mary Ethal Oct. 16, 1887 - Oct. 26, 1980 .... Block 34 #6
NEAL, M. G. no dates (deed to Acme Lodge Feb. 21, 1902) .... Block 15 #4
NEDDO, Jannett R. Aug. 9, 1930 - Jan. 19, 1984 .... Block 1 #7
NELSON, Christina M. 1880 - 1912 .... Block 5 #12
NELSON, Cinderella 1859 - 1952 .... Block 5 #12
NELSON, Laura L. Gonser 1913 - Dec. 26, 1935 .... Block 5 #12
NELSON, Nels 1864 - July 14, 1928 .... Block 5 #12
NICHOLLS, Harry n/d - Nov. 2, 1886 .... Block 16 #103
NICOLAI, Gustave N. 1851 - 1903 .... Block 25 #6
NIECGORSKI, John A. (So. 1/2)(deed to John & Gina Niecgorski 9/17/1971) .... Street 2 #31
NORTHWAY, Claude (No. 1/2) .... Block 5 #18
NOVAK, (deed to Frank Novak 10/30/1912) .... Block 5 #2
NUNNALLY, Eddie June 13, 1900 - Feb. 15, 1919 .... Block 18 #3
NUNNALLY, William F. 1857 - 1938 .... Block 18 #3

Pine Grove cemetery directory listing for Nagel

View north from the directory building is block 37, the Nagel plot 4 (center) is just in front of the tree, plot 12 is to the north at the end of the street.

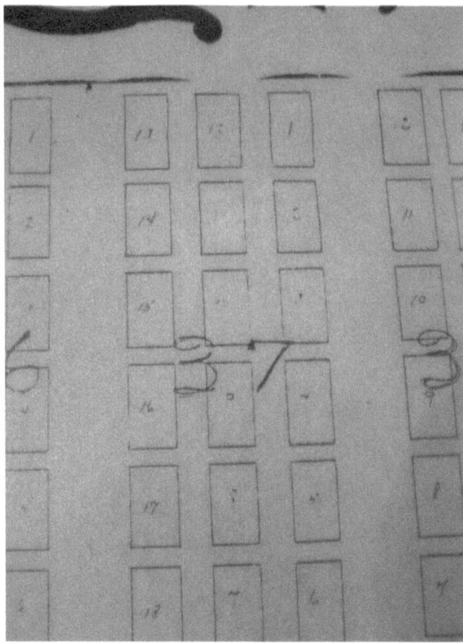

Block 37, plot 4 and plot 12

John Nagel Sr. 1883 – 1962, Barbara Nagel 1895 – 1994

John Nagel Jr. 1918 – 1975, Anna L. 1922 - 1960

Chapter 7 - John and Barbara Nagel's Descendants

Edna Nagel, 1944, at a Park in Spokane, about 10 miles north outside of Spokane, the Bowl and Pitcher Park

After High School graduation, during the war, Edna started working at Western Union in Spokane. It was the first time she went into Spokane by herself. They needed operators. She lived in Spokane with Johnny and Anna for a few months and then got reassigned to Los Angeles. She took the train from Spokane to LA with four other girls in September of 1943 (she was in LA for her 18th birthday). She signed up for four months. Edna kept a scrap book when she was in LA and still has it. She has a picture album from when she was young too.

Edna Nagel, taken in Los Angeles, 1944, 45
Before bike picture

She was engaged in LA to Dick Boswin. His mother was the house mother where they lived. He was a merchant marine. They went everywhere on the street car, no one had cars.

Edna couldn't give blood because she was anemic. Her friends called her "turnip" because you couldn't get blood out of a turnip.

There was no TV, they went to the radio programs and Hollywood shows every day off. After four months she came back to Spokane and lived at the WCA working for Western Union. She went back again to LA in 1945 and lived for another six months there working for Western Union again. She came back again to Spokane.

After bike picture, 2nd time down to Los Angeles,
1946, 47 after the war Edna Nagel
After polio, in 1946, Marie Hogan did Edna's hair
Taken at Baileys Studio in Spokane

On December 8th of 1946 in Spokane, Edna got polio and spent three and a half months in St. Luke's Hospital. She went back to Rathdrum and lived with Momma and Papa for several months because she still couldn't work. The polio affected her right leg and left arm. The doctor came in and examined her muscles and said she would not walk again: "this one won't come back". They thought she had appendicitis at first and she had an appendectomy. After the operation, she had a spinal tap to diagnose the Polio. Herb caught Polio two weeks later.

After the doctor left, Edna said to the nurse, "well, I can always walk with crutches." The nurse replied: "you dummy, how can you walk with crutches if you don't have any muscles in your arms?!"

Edna Nagel, taken in Rathdrum, summer of 1947 after polio, Little house built on farm about a mile outside of Rathdrum, little bunkhouse built for Hiennie and Dorothy Bentz

Edna was usually scared of her dad growing up; he would beat the kids for anything. He didn't say more than a hundred words to her growing up. At home with polio and living with him, he was determined to get her to walk again. He would get a cane and walk her around the yard. That's how she got walking again.

Edna Nagel, 1946 after polio, 1948?
In apartment in Spokane, working before she met Robert.

Chapter 8 - Edna and Robert Emmick

John Bird, Virginia Bird and their two girls, Edna, Robert,
Virginia is Roberts cousin, (Virginia Roberts, Verna and Anna Roberts daughter)
Taken at Virginia's home in Spokane.

In the fall of 1947, Edna started working again, this time at Hofius Ferris a caterpillar tractor seller. She did the bookkeeping. She met Robert while working there. Virginia, (on marriage certificate as witness) a friend of Edna's, was Robert's cousin. She invited Edna out to her house one day in Spokane to meet him. Robert was working for the State Highway Department doing manual labor out on the highway. They started going out together. He had been through college and law school but had not taken the bar exam yet. His mother did not want him to be an attorney. Edna talked him into taking the bar exam at the University of Washington. He went back to the U of W in Seattle and took a few refresher courses.

They decided to get married. He gave her an engagement ring (that Mary has now). When she took it into work everyone said "hold out your hand and show off your big ring."

MISS E. NAGEL WILL BE BRIDE

The engagement of Miss Edna Nagel of Spokane, daughter of Mrs. John Nagel of Rathdrum, Idaho, to Robert Emmick, son of Mr. and Mrs. E. F. Emmick of Olympia, is announced. The couple will be married Saturday in Spokane.

The bride-elect was graduated from Rathdrum high school and

Miss Edna Nagel

Kinman Business university. She has been with Hofius-Ferris Equipment company for the last seven years. Mr. Emmick was graduated from the University of Washington law school last June. They will make their home in Olympia.

Miss Nagel was guest of honor at a party Friday evening given by Mrs. Clifford Vawter and Mrs. H. Bird Wright, at the Vawter home, E1407 Eighteenth. She received gifts for her future kitchen.

Guests included for the affair were Mrs. Richard Hoefner, Mrs. Florence Hinton, Mrs. Verda Mae Perry, Mrs. Vern Roberts, Mrs. H. A. Teter, Mrs. Patricia Kathman, and the Misses Vinie Hoefner, Marie Hougen, Mildred Newkirk, Fern Lyon, Lucille Nelson. Miss Nagel's mother was unable to attend due to weather conditions.

Wedding announcement to Robert Emmick
Edna 24 years old, 1949

Robert took the bar exam. They got married on a Saturday, February 11th, 1950. When they got back to Olympia there was a telegram that day saying he had passed the bar. They went around the Olympic loop for their honeymoon, spending the first night in Aberdeen. Then they went up around the loop and spent the night in Port Angeles. It was the first time Edna had seen the Washington Ocean. She had seen the Pacific Ocean in California. Robert was just 28. Edna was pregnant right away. Rich was born 9 months and 13 days from the wedding, on November 24th. The doctor said that if he came early, he would put him in an incubator until he was nine months.

They had an apartment on 19th and Capital Way. They then moved to a small house at 1210 North Central near the old Emmick family home in Olympia.

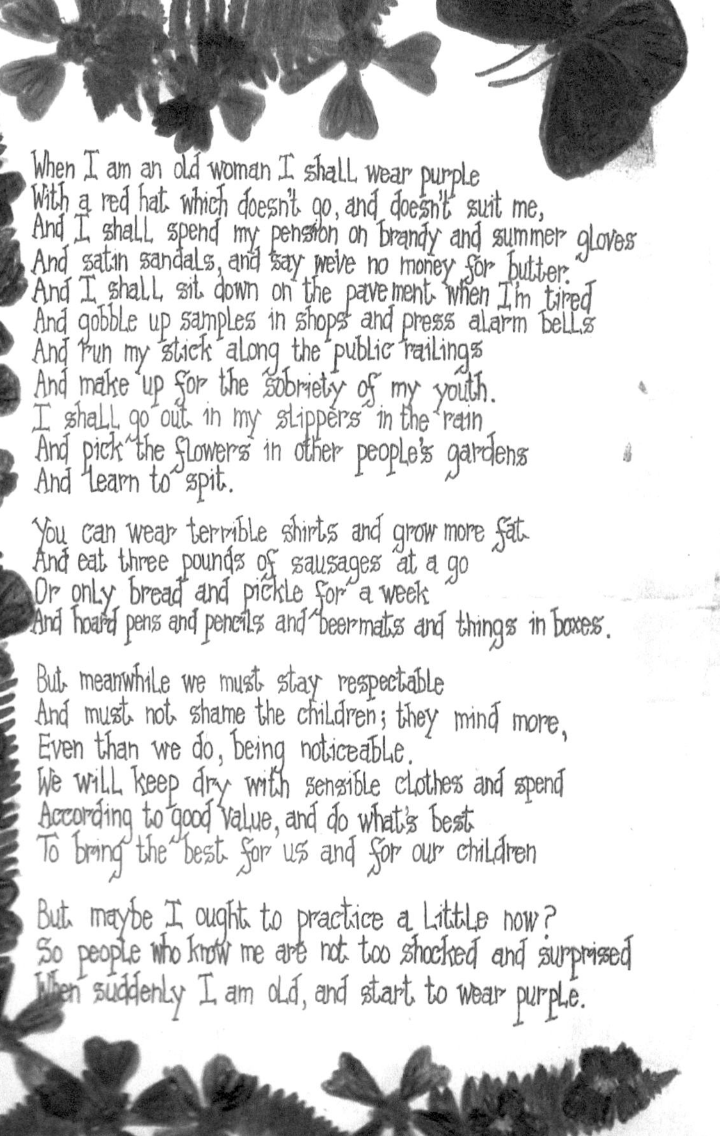
When I am an old woman I shall wear purple
With a red hat which doesn't go, and doesn't suit me,
And I shall spend my pension on brandy and summer gloves
And satin sandals, and say we've no money for butter.
And I shall sit down on the pavement when I'm tired
And gobble up samples in shops and press alarm bells
And run my stick along the public railings
And make up for the sobriety of my youth.
I shall go out in my slippers in the rain
And pick the flowers in other people's gardens
And learn to spit.

You can wear terrible shirts and grow more fat
And eat three pounds of sausages at a go
Or only bread and pickle for a week
And hoard pens and pencils and beermats and things in boxes.

But meanwhile we must stay respectable
And must not shame the children; they mind more,
Even than we do, being noticeable.
We will keep dry with sensible clothes and spend
According to good value, and do what's best
To bring the best for us and for our children

But maybe I ought to practice a little now?
So people who know me are not too shocked and surprised
When suddenly I am old, and start to wear purple.

Chapter 9 – Pictures

John and Barbara Nagel, in house in Rathdrum, see front door,
Ernie Harms was a sheriff up in San Point Idaho, David remembers him needing to duck down and turn his shoulders in order to come in this front door. He would explode into the room

Herby and Barbara, about 1959
This is before papa died, she hasn't cut her hair yet, she cuts her hair after papa died.
House in Rathdrum, living room

When papa died Barbara went down to her sister Arlene's in California. They went to Los Vegas. One morning Arlene woke up and couldn't find her. She found her down playing bingo at the bingo table.

Katherine Heuther, Barbara Nagel, Gertie Lindstrom holding Karen Lindstrom
Four generations
About 1947, at Linstrom's House in Otis Orchards. Five acres.

Gertie Linstrom, Anna Harms, Edna Emmick, Dorothy Bentz
1954, the old house on Dorothy's farm
Little girl might be Marilyn, back near porch

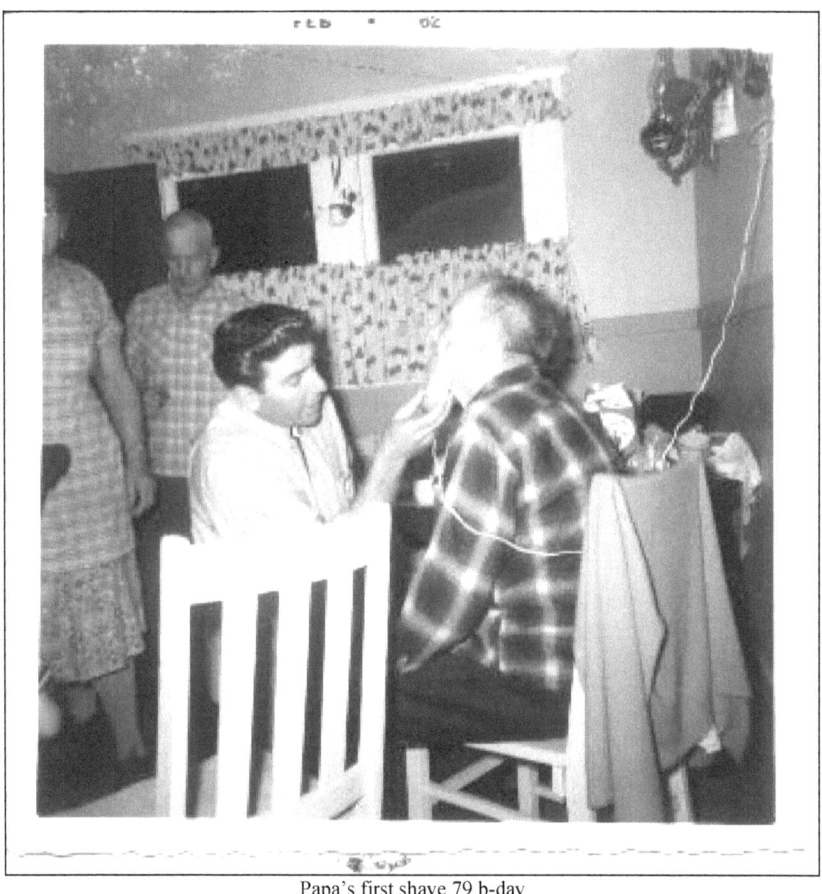

Papa's first shave 79 b-day
Papa died later that year at 79 years old.
Harold shaving John (papa) Nagel,
Momma (Barbara) and Walt Lindstrom in background
About 1961- 62

First row: Heinnie, Anna, Violet, Gertie, Sandy,
Top row, Auggie, Dorothy, Charlie, Barbara (grandma) Herby, Edna, Robert
Taken at park in Rathdrum for family reunion, about 1970-71, note the clothes

Anna, Charlie, Barbara, Herby, Edna
Gertie and Dorothy in front
About 1971

Anna, Gertie, Dorothy, Grandma (Barbara)
Grandma's trailer in Rathdrum, about 1980

Dorothy's girl, Barbara (mama) Rick or Steve's wife?) Bee (Harold's ex-wife holding kids) ? ?
Back row, Edna, Marilyn, Harold, , blank, Steve, Charlie, Violet, blank, Ed, Heine
Gertie in middle

Barbara, 1992-93

Barbara, Edna, Marilyn,
About 1975

Aunt Eva Hoefner, Barbara Nagel, Arlene
About 86 - 87

Barbara Nagel,
Late 1980s

Barbara Nagel, 1990's

Edna holding Heidi, Mary Emmick, David holding Rachel, Barbara Nagel, Nancy, Ed, Rich
Front, Marilyn, Hillary and Chris on chair
Barbara 75, Twin Lakes at Grandma's birthday celebration

Walter Paul Linstrom, "Lindy"
Taken recently

Herb, Barbara and John Nagel
Oct. 1955
By the house in Rathdrum

Barbara Nagel

Barbara, John, Johnnie and Anna, Charlie and Violet,
Anna harms, Gertie, Mr. and Mrs. Harms,

Barbara Nagel holding?

Rich and Nancy Emmick

Chapter 10 – Remembering Edna

On September 26th the family gathered to remember Edna. Ed arranged to use the Paulson's beach house on Hartstine Island and even bought wave runners to have fun. Getting the family together to have fun is how Edna wanted to be remembered.

STRAIGHT

STRAIGHT LINE

Kawasaki
WN9937RC

Appendix

Descendants of Ludwig HUETHER - Fifth Generation

58. **Carl NAGEL** (Barbara HUETHER , Paul , Paul , Ludwig Jacob) was born 11 Jun 1919 in Lind, WA. He died 5 Nov 1991.
Carl married **Violet Florence HARMS** on 26 Jun 1943. Violet was born 5 Mar 1926.
They had the following children:

+ 77 M i **Carl Ernest NAGEL** was born 23 Sep 1945.
78 M ii **Henry John NAGEL** was born 25 Jan 1947.
Henry married (1) **Barbara KING** on 12 Aug 1967. The marriage ended in divorce.
Henry also married (2) **Patricia Maureen PEDERSON** on 21 Sep 1970. Patricia was born 23 Nov 1949.
79 M iii **Claude Joe NAGEL** was born 7 Mar 1948. He died 12 May 1948.

59. **Gertrude Lydia NAGEL** "Gertie" (Barbara HUETHER , Paul , Paul , Ludwig Jacob) was born 28 May 1921 in Lind, WA. She died 17 Feb 2005 in Idaho.
Gertie married **Walter LINDSTROM** on 7 Apr 1940.
They had the following children:

+ 80 M i **Walter Paul LINDSTROM** was born 18 Aug 1941.
81 F ii **Karen Kay LINDSTROM** was born 18 May 1945.
Karen married **Karl KRUGER** on 18 Mar 1978.

60. **Anna Freida NAGEL** (Barbara HUETHER , Paul , Paul , Ludwig Jacob) was born 27 Mar 1923 in Lind, WA.
Anna married **August Eugene HARMS** "Aggy" on 19 Jul 1941. Aggy was born 27 May 1919.
They had the following children:

+ 82 M i **Robert Eugene HARMS** was born 4 May 1942.
83 F ii **Agusta Jean HARMS** was born 25 Feb 1944.
+ 84 F iii **Barbara Ann HARMS** was born 4 Feb 1946.
85 F iv **Katherine Ruby HARMS** was born 25 Apr 1949.
86 M v **John August HARMS** was born 2 Nov 1950.

61. **Edna Ottile NAGEL** (Barbara HUETHER , Paul , Paul , Ludwig Jacob) was born 12 Oct 1925 in Lind, WA. She died 13 Aug 2010 in Tacoma, WA.
Edna married **Robert Edward EMMICK** on 11 Feb 1950. Robert was born 29 Mar 1922 in Bremerton, Kitsap, Washington. He died 1980 and was buried in Veteran's Cemetery, Portland, Oregon.
They had the following children:

+ 87 M i **Richard EMMICK** was born 24 Nov 1950.

+ 88 F ii **Marilyn EMMICK** was born 25 Apr 1952.

+ 89 M iii **David John EMMICK** was born 4 Oct 1955.

90 M iv **Edward Robert EMMICK** was born 26 Oct 1958.

62. **Harold NAGEL** (Barbara HUETHER , Paul , Paul , Ludwig Jacob) was born 19 Apr 1927 in Lind, Washington. He died 26 Feb 2005 in Idaho.
Harold married **Beatrice MCNURLIN**.
They had the following children:

+ 91 M i **Harold Stephen NAGEL** was born 24 Nov 1949.

+ 92 M ii **Rickie Lane NAGEL** was born 12 Jan 1950.

63. **Dorothy Madeline NAGEL** (Barbara HUETHER , Paul , Paul , Ludwig Jacob) was born 9 Jul 1929.
Dorothy married **Henry BENTZ** on 29 Mar 1947. Henry was born 4 Aug.
They had the following children:

+ 93 F i **Janet BENTZ** was born 16 Sep 1949.

94 F ii **Jackie BENTZ** was born 13 Aug 1954.

+ 95 F iii **Shirley BENTZ** was born 10 Apr 1957.

96 F iv **Sheryl BENTZ** was born 28 Jun 1959.

64. **Herbert NAGEL** "Herby" (Barbara HUETHER , Paul , Paul , Ludwig Jacob) was born 19 Aug 1931 in Sprague, Washington.
Herby married **Sandra Jill VONHOSTEEN** on 29 Jun. Sandra was born 30 Mar 1936.
They had the following children:

97 F i **Tamara Jeanne NAGEL** was born 14 Feb 1955.

98 F ii **Tanya Jayne NAGEL** was born 7 Apr 1957.
Tanya married **John David KIRSCH** "Jack" on 7 Jul 1979. Jack was born 8 Feb 1954.

99 F iii **Traci Jill NAGEL** was born 23 Aug 1964.

100 F iv **Triana Jo NAGEL** was born 1 Dec 1967.

Descendants of Ludwig HUETHER - Sixth Generation

77. **Carl Ernest NAGEL** "Ernie" (Carl NAGEL , Barbara HUETHER , Paul , Paul , Ludwig Jacob) was born 23 Sep 1945.
Ernie married (1) **Linda Joy PARKER** on 27 Jul 1968. The marriage ended in divorce. Linda was born 15 Jan 1952.
They had the following children:

101 F i **Shawna Lee NAGEL** was born 9 Nov 1969.

102 M ii **Carl Ernest NAGEL Junior** was born 4 Jan 1971.

Ernie also married (2) **Susan Ann Lee NEEDS** on 16 May 1975. Susan was born 29 Mar 1947.
They had the following children:

103 M iii **Charlie Russell NAGEL** was born 24 Aug 1977 in Sandpoint, ID.

104 M iv **Richard Allen NEEDS** was born 18 Oct 1967.

105 F v **Crystal Anne NEEDS** was born 13 Oct 1969.

80. **Walter Paul LINDSTROM** (Gertrude Lydia NAGEL , Barbara HUETHER , Paul , Paul , Ludwig Jacob) was born 18 Aug 1941.
Walter married **Nancy Paulette JOHNSTON (FOWLER)** on 1 Dec 1973. Nancy was born 16 Mar 1942.
They had the following children:

106 M i **James Douglas FOWLER** was born 12 Jul 1966.

107 F ii **Kimberley Sue FOWLER** was born 15 Nov 1968.

108 M iii **Rodd Erik LINDSTROM** was born 12 May 1975.

82. **Robert Eugene HARMS** (Anna Freida NAGEL , Barbara HUETHER , Paul , Paul , Ludwig Jacob) was born 4 May 1942.
Robert married (1) **Thelma HOWARD**. The marriage ended in divorce.
They had the following children:

109 M i **Charlie HARMS** was born 5 Jul 1965.

110 M ii **Robert HARMS** was born 20 Sep 1966.

Robert also married (2) **Mary KING**. The marriage ended in divorce.
They had the following children:

111 F iii **Susann HARMS** was born 21 Jun.

Robert also married (3) **Linda** on 22 Sep. Linda was born 6 Feb.
They had the following children:

112 M iv **Robbie Jason HARMS** was born 23 Jul 1975.

113 F v **Jinny Lee HARMS** was born 22 Jun.

84. **Barbara Ann HARMS** (Anna Freida NAGEL , Barbara HUETHER , Paul , Paul , Ludwig Jacob) was born 4 Feb 1946.

Barbara married (1) **James TEALE**. The marriage ended in divorce.
They had the following children:

114 M i **James Robert TEALE** was born 26 Apr 1965.

Barbara also married (2) **Richard Mark SCOTT** on 20 Apr 1968. Richard was born 5 May 1941.
They had the following children:

115 M ii **David Michael SCOTT** was born 13 Feb 1963.

116 F iii **Lisa Jean SCOTT** was born 9 Mar 1964.

117 M iv **Mark James SCOTT** was born 28 Jan 1966.

118 F v **Kimberly Kay SCOTT** was born 10 May 1970.

87. **Richard EMMICK** (Edna Ottile NAGEL , Barbara HUETHER , Paul , Paul , Ludwig Jacob) was born 24 Nov 1950.
Richard married **Nancy JONES**.
They had the following children:

119 M i **Christopher EMMICK** "Chris" was born 29 Mar 1980.

120 M ii **Jeffrey EMMICK** "Jeff" was born 12 Sep 1983.

88. **Marilyn EMMICK** (Edna Ottile NAGEL , Barbara HUETHER , Paul , Paul , Ludwig Jacob) was born 25 Apr 1952.
Marilyn married **Steven SHULER**.
They had the following children:

\+ 121 F i **Hilary SHULER** was born 23 Jan 1975.

122 F ii **Heidi SHULER** was born 6 Nov 1981 in Tacoma, Washington.

89. **David John EMMICK** (Edna Ottile NAGEL , Barbara HUETHER , Paul , Paul , Ludwig Jacob) was born 4 Oct 1955 in Tacoma, Pierce, Washington and was christened in Fircrest Methodist Church, Fircrest, Washington.
David married **Mary Kay JUDGE** on 15 Aug 1982 in St. Vincent De Paul Church, Federal Way, King, Washington. Mary was born 2 Oct 1956 in Harvey, Cook, Ill.
They had the following children:

123 F i **Rachel Katherine EMMICK** was born 23 May 1983 in Group Health Hospital, Redmond, King County, Washington.

124 F ii **Rebecca Mary EMMICK** was born 21 Aug 1985 in Seattle, King County, Washington.

91. **Harold Stephen NAGEL** (Harold NAGEL , Barbara HUETHER , Paul , Paul , Ludwig Jacob) was born 24 Nov 1949 in Spirit Lake, Idaho.
Harold married **Sheryl MATHESON** on 20 Jun 1971. Sheryl was born 28 May 1953.
They had the following children:

125 M i **Michael Travis NAGEL** was born 18 Dec 1971.

126 F ii **Heather Dawn NAGEL** was born 8 Jun 1975.

127 M iii **Justin Patrick NAGEL** was born 7 May 1978.

92. **Rickie Lane NAGEL** (Harold NAGEL , Barbara HUETHER , Paul , Paul , Ludwig Jacob) was born 12 Jan 1950 in Spirit Lake, Idaho.
Rickie married **Beverly BUCK** on 13 Jun 1969. Beverly was born 30 Dec 1950.
They had the following children:
128 i **Lynnel Dionne NAGEL** was born 28 Dec 1969.
93. **Janet BENTZ** (Dorothy Madeline NAGEL , Barbara HUETHER , Paul , Paul , Ludwig Jacob) was born 16 Sep 1949.
Janet married **James KLAUE** on 15 Jun 1966.
They had the following children:
129 F i **Wendy KLAUE** was born 28 Aug 1967.
130 M ii **Scotty KLAUE** was born 20 Oct 1969.
95. **Shirley BENTZ** (Dorothy Madeline NAGEL , Barbara HUETHER , Paul , Paul , Ludwig Jacob) was born 10 Apr 1957.
Shirley married **Robert E. EDWARDS** on 4 Oct 1975. Robert was born 6 Feb 1952.
They had the following children:
131 F i **Miranda Deanne EDWARDS** was born 7 Jul 1977.

Huether Name Genealogy

It is common to add an "e" after the "ü" to Anglicize the name making Hüther the likely German spelling.

Speculative: One family member found information on Ancestry.com that Johann Ludwig Jacob Huether was the son of Georgius Phillipus Huetter born 1764 in Hungary. His wife was Christiana Meiss. Georgius's father was Christianus Huetter and wife Marium Elizabetham Diehlin. Christianus's father was Georgius Henricus Huetter and wife Anna Margaretha Freyler. That would take it back 3 more generations if that is indeed true.

From an internet search "Our Velten & Ashe Families, Genealogies of our German and Scotch-Irish Families"
http://www.dvelten.net/vaf-o/i38.htm#s599

> **Johannes Hüther** died before Apr 1828
> Mother: Elisabetha Buchheit born 1763
> Johannes Hüther was born in Germany. Johannes married Elisabetha Buchheit born 1763, daughter of Johann Georg Buchheit and Margaretha Schön, in Germany. Johannes died before April 1828 in Germany.

Children

i.Elisabetha Hüther

ii.Heinrich Hüther+ b. 15 Oct 1790

Heinrich Hüther was born on 15 October 1790 in Paulengrund, Kusel, Rheinland-Pfalz, Germany. He was the son of Johannes Hüther and Elisabetha Buchheit. Heinrich married Anna Maria Buser on 2 November 1815 in Kübelberg, Kusel, Rheinland-Pfalz, Germany.

The above may be a place to search records for our line.

There is also a Johann Adam Hüther (Schultheiß)

- Baptism 20 July 1680
- Died 6 February 1755 - Reifenberg, Pirmasens (Land),Rheinland-Pfalz,Deutschland,66507,D

Pre-1833 Odessa Area Births (D. Wahl)

Published by the Odessa Digital Library - 11 Nov 2001
http://pixel.cs.vt.edu/library/odessa.html

The following index data has been taken from the four Church Family Books for Freudental and Peterstal in the Odessa area from 1841 through 1880. This index is only defined to contain those who were born prior to 1833 (when the Annual St Petersburg Reports start). Translated copies of these four family books are available individually (each family book) in the bookstore at GRHS. For those who resided in these two villages during this time frame, whose birth was after this 1833 mark, see the indexes available for each family book at the bookstore on the GRHS homepage. It is the intent of the GRHS Clearing House to supplement the St Petersburg

References:
A 1841-1860 Freudental Church Family Book
B 1841-1860 Peterstal Church Family Book
C 1861-1880 Freudental Church Family Book
D 1861-1880 Peterstal Church Family Book
http://www.rootsweb.ancestry.com/~ukrgs/odessa/odesp33b.txt

Last, First	BORN D/M	BORN Year	Page	Ref	Remarks
Hochstaedtler, Christina			257	A	
Hoffmann, Friedrich			91	B	
Hoffmann, Ludwig Friedrich			84	B	
Hofmann, Philippina			47	B	
Huebner, Georg Christoph	3 Jul	1805	110	A	
Huebner, Georg Christoph	3 Jul	1805	40	C	
Huether, Barbara	1 Nov	1823	138	B	
Huether, Elisabeth Margaretha	26 Feb	1833	47	A	
Huether, Elisabetha Margareth	26 Feb	1833	85	B	
Huether, Eva Elisabetha	1 Sep	1831	85	B	
Huether, Georg Nicolaus	27 Jan	1827	85	B	
Huether, Georg Peter	3 Apr	1828	85	B	
Huether, Georg Peter	3 Apr	1828	33	D	
Huether, Johannes	21 Aug	1825	85	B	
Huether, Johannes	21 Aug	1825	96	B	
Huether, Ludwig	3 Apr	1828	85	B	
Huether, Maria Barbara	1 Nov	1823	85	B	
Huether, Nicolaus	27 Nov	1827	75	B	
Huether, Nicolaus	27 Jan	1827	95	B	
Huether, Paul	6 Feb	1830	73	B	
Huether, Paul	6 Feb	1830	85	B	
Huther, Elisabetha Margaretha	26 Feb	1833	17	C	
Ottmar, Christina	24 Apr	1792	186	A	Pfaff
Ottmar, Christine	24 Apr	1782	70	C	Pfaff

Peterstal - 1848 Village History (GRHS)

http://www.odessa3.org/collections/history/link/petersal.txt

Published by the Odessa Digital Library - 1 Jun 1996
http://www.odessa3.org

Notes: Please see the Introduction to the Village History Project for additional information.

This particular Village History was published in the English form in Joseph S. Height's book "Homesteaders on the Steppe". There is much more data contained in this book concerning this area and our German Russian ancestors who lived there. As this file is placed on the Internet, the book is still available from the GRHS (copyright holder).

PETERSTAL

Forever precious you will be to our posterity,
Brief documentary of our dear Peterstal!
Long after everyone in this community
Will have turned to dust, as must we all,
Our remembered past will bring a shared delight
To our descendants on a dreary winter night.
With purer, nobler striving they will emulate
To do their best for their own children's sake.
And on him who bade me write this resume
May God's blessing rest eternally!

Foreword

Since the founding of our colony the second generation has already grown to manhood, but no one thought of the idea of writing down for future generations an account of those events that have had an impact on the destinies of our colonists. We are, therefore, deeply indebted to the president of the Colonists' Welfare Committee, His Excellency State Councilor von Hahn, for enjoining us to fulfill our sacred duty to posterity by "preserving for them our remembered history and satisfying their desire to know what events happened in the past."

Dearest descendants! In spirit we envision you gathered together in dreary winter evenings, eager to read and discover how the colony was founded, how it developed, and in what condition it now finds itself. Let us then cheerfully set to work and compose a brief survey of our history, with the prayerful wish that the Almighty may graciously preserve our new fatherland, with its government officials and colonial administrators, in perpetual peace.

I. The Founding of the Colony

In the beginning of the 19. century, when the general proclamation to would-be colonists was issued in the Kingdom of Hungary, where our forefathers from Wuerttemberg and the Rhineland had already been settled as farmers, our parents decided to emigrate to Russia. They arrived here in the summer of 1805 and built themselves wattled huts of reed and grass. The following year the government completed the construction of houses made of stamped earth or sun-dried clay blocks. The settlers were also granted a loan to enable them to purchase needed farm equipment, livestock, and seed for field and garden.
Every year the colony has paid off 428 rubles of this loan, but there is still an outstanding debt of 9,978 rubles. From the day the immigrants crossed the frontier until they were completely established, the Crown also provided them with so-called "day money", wherewith they were able to buy the necessary food rations.

II. The Immigration

Our parents traveled together in groups of 10-12 families, without a special guide or conductor. Some families came alone, but were also established in the Liebental district.

Only three families brought with them a sizable sum of money. The rest had no significant funds. The former were therefore able to plow and sow and raise livestock as they pleased, for the steppe was vast and grass was abundant.
They obtained good harvests and raised fine cattle and sheep. The poorer immigrants were eager, as far as possible, to follow their example, and devoted all their resources to farming. They lived frugally on barley gruel and potatoes. They dressed simply and were content to wear rawhide wrappers on their feet, instead of boots. But in due course they made such progress that they could afford better food and finer clothes.

There were, however, also some thoughtless people who cared little about morality, agriculture, or animal husbandry. They enticed others into drinking and frivolity, and ended up in an abject state of poverty.

Because the colonists were unacquainted with the local conditions of the soil and the climate, little progress was made in the first ten years, despite good crops and extensive grazing lands. In later years the pioneer settlers had to give some of their land to the landless artisans and day laborers, so that each family retained only 50 of the original 60 dessiatines.

In the beginning 40-50 families were settled here. Others arrived in subsequent years, until, in 1816/17, the completed settlement consisted of 61 families. No orchards or vineyards were planted in the early years. Indeed, the people were firmly convinced that neither trees nor vines could be grown in this region.

III. The Location of the Colony

Peterstal is located on the Baraboi river, immediately south of the colony of Freudental, and about 26 versts from Odessa. The single village street, consisting of two rows of houses and an avenue of acacia and elm trees, runs parallel to the river. West of the street, on the other side of the river, is a beautiful hill with green grass, vines, and fruit trees. On the summit, which provides a fine view of the colony, the settlers built their village church.

IV. The Naming of the Colony

The name Peterstal is attributed to an amusing little incident. One day, while the chief mayor of the Liebental district was visiting with the local village mayor whose name was Peter, the latter called his beadle, also named Peter, to deliver a message to a neighboring colonist of the same name. Struck by this coincidence, the chief mayor is said to have exclaimed: "Hier ist ein wahres Peterstal!" (You have here a veritable valley of Peters).

V. The Boundaries of the Colony

The land belonging to the colony is bounded on the east and north by the colony of Josephstal; on the south by Freudental; on the west by Mariental and the Russian village of Majak. The land area amounts to 2,994 dessiatines of level terrain, which is traversed on the east side by the Akershi valley, and on the west by the Baraboi with its lateral valleys.

VI. The Soil

Our steppe has black fertile soil everywhere, except on the west bank of the Baraboi and its four dales, where the ground has a heavy content of sand and gravel. The Agricultural Society claims that this western terrain is definitely suitable for the production of certain trees, such as walnut, acacia and mulberry, but so far nothing has been done to demonstrate this possibility.

VII. Vineyards, Orchards, and Tree Plantations

Upon injunctions issued by the authorities we began to plant fruit trees, vines, and mulberries at the end of the first decade. However, despite all efforts expended on them, the trees did not thrive, largely because of the saltpeter in the soil and the recurrence of dry summers. Because of the slow and stunted growth of the trees, the colonists soon lost confidence and interest in this branch of agriculture and began to neglect it. Our gardeners soon became convinced that the climate of the steppe was only suitable for nomads and gypsies. Some said, "I shall plow down my vines and uproot my trees, and begin to sow rye or barley. From the income of the field I shall afford to buy myself a fine woolen coat."

It was not until 1840 that a new attempt was made to grow trees. The recently appointed superintendent of German colonies, His Excellency von Hahn, together with the district officials, organized an agricultural society in the Liebental area. This society was requested to exert every possible effort to improve the gardens and vineyards, and to establish new plantations of trees. Its president was the Freudental colonist Konrad Bechthold, whose research of agricultural matters and tree-growing in this district will remain unforgotten.

To be sure, the superintendent and the society had a hard time trying to overcome the people's prejudice and skepticism. But the undertaking took a new turn when von Hahn simply issued orders that "trees had to be planted." Though the colonists remained skeptical and reluctant, they obeyed the order. After seven years many of the colonists were vying with each other, to see who could develop the nicest orchards and produce the finest trees. In 1845 the two sons of a local widow who owned a large vineyard, devised a method of channeling run-off water and storing it in small reservoirs, so that they could irrigate the vines during the dry summer. As a result, in the dry year of 1846, their vineyard was in a more flourishing state than the best one in a wet year. Everyone admired it, but apparently no one thought of emulating the method. However, most of the present inhabitants did try to follow the instructions of the agricultural society and have thereby managed to improve their plantations. In the late fall of 1846, ditches were made on both sides of the road leading to Freudental, and an avenue of trees was planted on the banks of earth.

VIII. Wheat and Grain Farming

Our colony owes its prosperity chiefly to the production of wheat and other grain. In the first decade the biggest farmer here was the village mayor, a man named Pflug (plow!), who sowed 18-20 chetvert (95-100 bushels) of grain every year, for which achievement he was awarded a silver medal by the Czar.
The other colonists sowed, on the average, only 18 to 24 bushels a year.

On the fertile virgin soil of the steppe the colonists were generally able to produce good harvests, and our parents would have begun farming on an extensive scale, had it not been because of obstacles they could not surmount.
In those years farm laborers were not easily available. The prices paid for grain were low. Moreover, it was almost impossible to obtain the necessary wood and iron for the construction of farm implements. Finally, the colonists did not realize that only one

day was needed to haul a load of wheat to Odessa, sell it, make the necessary purchases, and be home again before nightfall.

In the beginning of the second decade, as more people began to settle in the neighborhood, farm laborers became more available and many a colonist now had several children of working age. The price of wheat became unusually high, so that the colonists were able to market their grain in Odessa at great profit.
Until the end of the decade the most productive grain was winter wheat. After that the soil began to lose some of its earlier vigor and fertility. Nevertheless, no attempts were made to preserve and improve the depleted soil.
On the contrary, the colonists continued to plow and harrow the fields year after year and to sow more and more grain, in the hope of getting larger crops. The result was that the farmers had to pick the stunted grain by hand, because it could not be reaped by scythe or sickle. Indeed, the harvest was so meager that it scarcely sufficed for livestock fodder, and the farmers had to work on the fields of the Glueckstal colony in order to earn their bread and the necessary seed grain. After the land was allowed to lie fallow from time to time, it again recovered and continued to bear good harvests in the third decade.

Through the efforts of his Excellency von Hahn, in cooperation with the officials of the Liebental district and the agricultural society, a good deal of light has been shed on the problem of grain farming. The farmers have recognized the value of summer fallow and the rotation of the crops.
Consequently, despite the recent 8 years of drought, the colony is rapidly moving toward greater prosperity in many respects.

IX. Animal Husbandry

Next to grain farming, the colony owes its prosperity to the raising of livestock. It is a well-known fact that livestock does well in this district and that its quality can be improved with proper care. However, it has happened that outbreaks of livestock epidemics have carried off two-thirds of our herds, but these losses were again made good in three years.

Although the pioneer settlers had received from the Crown only oxen as draught animals, they were not used very long but replaced by horses. Soon most farmers had four horses, and some had eight. The colonists preferred to use horses, because they were able to work faster and no epidemics had ever broken out among them. Moreover, they always sold at a higher price than other livestock. For several years the government has helped us to make improvements in the breeding of horses.

Our parents would have liked to raise sheep, but they claimed that there was not enough grazing land available. Today the colonists admit that every farmer could keep a few sheep without causing any harm to the steppe land. Families would also find it easy to obtain their own supply of wool needed for clothing.

The Liebental officials and the agricultural society are studying the possibility of raising clover, in order to increase the present herd of sheep.

X. Crafts and Trades

In the second decade only one family supported itself by operating a pottery. Through hard work and thrift it has prospered so well that it is now a member of the merchants' guild in Odessa and the owner of a profitable business. From the beginning of the colony it was shown that blacksmiths, wainwrights, cobblers, and coopers who were hardworking could make a good livelihood in their special craft. The day laborer, who is so necessary for our colony, can also earn a good income and enjoy a good life, without having to ruin his body through excessive work.

Already in the second decade, the government had planned to establish a silk industry and ordered the colonists to establish mulberry plantations. This was done, even though the settlers had neither the interest nor the knowledge for such an enterprise. Nevertheless, mulberry trees are still being planted by order of the agricultural society. Perhaps our descendants will be more successful in this field of endeavor than their forefathers were.

Apiculture, probably a very promising enterprise in the Odessa area, was completely neglected by our parents. In our village there is only one colonist who has several bee hives. The agricultural society, however, is seeking to spread more enlightenment in this branch of village industry.

XI. Private Dwellings

When our parents arrived, the steppe hereabouts was completely uninhabited. Only here and there in the valleys and on the plain one could see the ruins of lowly dwellings where Tatars were supposed to have been living. That these houses were inhabited by an uncultured race is quite obvious from their irregular and wretched construction, and the large piles of ashes nearby. Since these tumble-down dwellings were no longer habitable, the government built new ones for the settlers. In the first decade there was no thought of building regular houses, but in the second decade the colonists began to improve the old dwellings and build new ones. In the third and fourth decades most of the old houses were replaced by new ones, with sizable well-furnished rooms, cellars, and adjoining sheds and barns.

XII. Community Buildings

In the first few years there was no school, prayer hall, community hall, or storage granary. Soon a schoolhouse was built which was to serve all community needs for some time. On Sundays church services were held there and on weekdays it served as a school, a court room, and as a town hall. The attic was used to store provisions until, in 1820, a storage granary was constructed.

In 1836 we began the construction of the existing community buildings. Since the little schoolhouse had become too small to accommodate either the schoolchildren or the Sunday congregation, the community discussed the possibility of building a church. But the communal cash on hand amounted to a mere 7 silver rubles and 43 kopeks, and the colony was still so badly in arrears with its payment of the Crown loan, the unpaid taxes, and the orphans' fund, that its total indebtedness amounted to 5,000 silver rubles.

Nevertheless, the community engaged an architect, and the church was completed in 1837 at a total cost of 4,000 silver rubles. After the harvest of that same year this sum was paid off, and also the outstanding debts. The attractive church with steeple was also provided with interior furnishings, and the young people contributed to the purchase of a bell.

A few years later we erected a spacious schoolhouse, purchased a house for the mayor's office, enlarged the storage granary, and built barns for the communal breeding stock.

XIII. The Schoolmasters

From the beginning our schools were poorly provided with teachers. The cause of this was that they were hired as cheaply as possible. At the present time the situation has changed completely. Only those men who have been examined by the pastors are now engaged as schoolmasters, and they are paid an adequate salary. Upon the injunction of the authorities the children are now sent to school regularly, and are given an education in the service of God and their community.

XIV. Unfavorable Events

a. Crop failures.
Complete crop failure occurred in 1824 and 1833. In the first instance we were still able to earn our bread and seed grain, and fodder for our livestock, by working in the colony of Glueckstal. However, in 1833, things looked much darker and we were compelled to apply for aid from the colonial administration, and received money, bread, and seed grain. The entire loan, designated by the term "Hilfsgelder", was repaid in 1837. Although we had many other dry years, especially in the forties, we were still able to make regular payments on our Crown loan and the annual taxes.

b. Insects and rodents.
Since 1840 we have had a series of dry years which produced a spawn of bugs and caterpillars that caused a great deal of damage to the grain crops and the fruit trees. The wheatfields also were frequently ravaged by the so-called suslik, the steppe gopher.

c. Locusts and the so-called Prussiki.
These also caused great devastation in our fields in the beginning of the third decade. They appeared again in 1847, and completely destroyed our fields of maize. The prussiki, grasshoppers, have

also appeared frequently, but through the efforts of the agricultural society they are destroyed in their breeding grounds.

d. Hail.
The only hailstorm to sweep through this colony was that of 1844, which completely destroyed several grainfields.

e. Frost.
Hoar frost struck our vineyards and orchards several times. On April 17-18 of the year 1848 we had such a severe frost that the grapevine shoots and the leaves of the acacia and mulberry trees were frozen.

f. Fires.
A fire broke out in 1845 but consumed only one house. The owner, who was blameless, was compensated for his loss by the Fire Insurance Fund.

g. Livestock epidemics.
We have had four epidemics here, each of which carried off two-thirds of our herds, and impoverished many a family for several years.

h. Floods.
The Baraboi flooded several times. The most disastrous flood was that of February, 1845, which caused damage amounting to 1,703 silver rubles. The agricultural society is planning to provide flood control by building several dams. The existing large Baraboi dam above the village holds such a large quantity of water that we can water our cattle even throughout the driest summer.

i. Diseases.
God be praised, our colony has not been afflicted by any epidemic or contagious diseases. Indeed, we are in a flourishing condition, with a present population of 351 males and 338 females. One couple is still living that has a son of sixty-three and many great-grandchildren. In 1832, when cholera was raging in Odessa, we also had a few cases, but fortunately no one died.

General Retrospect

If we consider the good fortune we have enjoyed here since the beginning, and how, despite reverses and setbacks, we have been making substantial progress during the forties, we must conclude: "These are the wise dispensations of God who always does what is best for man." For, if we had not received crop failures as well as bountiful harvests, disaster as well as good fortune, what would have happened to morality and religion? With recurring change of fortune, our colonists came to realize that thrift and economy can be rewarding. Formerly the head of a family used to spend 60 silver rubles on wedding festivities for his child, and 20-25 rubles for baptismal feasts.
Nowadays, a wedding costs no more than a christening, and this can be celebrated with an outlay of 5 silver rubles.

The same is true of the trips to Odessa. Formerly the colonists thought it was necessary to stay overnight, in order to sell their products and purchase the household necessities. But now that our colonists have learned to economize, they set out at two in the morning, take care of all their business in the city, and are back home at three in the afternoon. To be sure, our colonial administrators and village officials have played their part in this important change, for they have ceaselessly striven to maintain good moral standards in the colony. How difficult their task must have been in the pioneer years, when the colonists, while enjoying the freedom of Russia in full measure, imagined that no one could interfere with their liberties. Fortunately, Heaven itself came to the aid of the authorities. Let us suppose that we had enjoyed bountiful crops year after year and had to suffer no misfortunes through crop failure, grasshoppers, epidemics and hailstorms, truly most of the colonists would still be living in their primitive clay-huts, and the colony as a whole would not have made any progress. We would have no vineyards, no orchards, no plantations of trees. All the former good harvests would have been squandered, and if we now had a couple of crop failures, we could scarcely survive. Why are we now able to pay our current taxes and the annual assessment on the Crown loan? And why, on the other hand, are there still unpaid arrears from former years when crops were good? We have clearly indicated the answer in earlier paragraphs.

We revert to the problem of agriculture. Since all of our land has been tilled and no more grassland is available for our steadily increasing herds, our colonists have had to lease many fields from our Russian neighbors. But now this land is also becoming depleted, and the question arises, how will it be possible in the future to improve the economy of the colony, particularly in view of the fact that its population is constantly increasing.

Every colonist here is firmly convinced that no better land than ours can be found anywhere, not even in Germany. The only thing that is lacking, is rain. And yet, we have frequent precipitation of rain and snow every year. If only the water that runs off into the sea could be retained for the benefit of our good land, the problem would be solved! Of course, this water would have to be conserved not only in ponds and depressions but also on level and hilly terrain. If this were done, our colonists, ten years from now, would not change places with the happiest inhabitants of the earth. Indeed, we would have here a foretaste of the heavenly Eden, especially if the colonists continued to cultivate their vineyards and orchards, and market their produce at Odessa in untold quantity.

For this very purpose His Excellency, with the co-operation of the district officials of Liebental, organized an agricultural society which is directing its constant attention to the improvement of the colony and seeking to discover sound solutions to all agricultural problems.

Epilogue

Russian land,
Sweet fatherland,
Where we colonists live in security!
O pledge that we prize
And recognize,
Let us serve with faithful zeal and industry.
Lord God,
Sustaining all,
Protect the crown of our Czar,
Whenever danger threatens,
Near or far.
Give him, O Lord,
We implore,
Faithful councilors and wise.
Grant, O Lord,
That as of yore
They look upon our colonies with gracious eyes.
And today,
As always,
May our life be devoted to God and our new Fatherland.

The original signed by:
Mayor: Schopp
Assessors: Klabe, Bauer.
Village deputies: Johannes Deifel, Friedrich Becker,
Adam Ziegler, and some members of the community.
Village clerk: J. Ulrich Roduner (author)

Scanned by Dale Lee Wahl
Coordinated with GRHS Village Research Clearing House
Coordinated with AHSGR/GRHS Translation Committee Chairman

Freudental - 1848 Village History (GRHS)

http://www.odessa3.org/collections/history/link/freudtal.txt

The Huethers found in Freudental are likely there from Peterstal through marriage or re-settlement.

Published by the Odessa Digital Library - 1 Jun 1996
http://www.odessa3.org

Notes: Please see the Introduction to the Village History Project for additional information.

This particular Village History was published in the English form inJoseph S. Height's book "Homesteaders on the Steppe". There is much more data contained in this book concerning this area and our German Russian ancestors who lived there. As this file is placed on the Internet, the book is still available from the GRHS (copyright holder).

FREUDENTAL

1. The immigrant settlers began the establishment of the colony of Freudental in 1806, and it was completed in 1807 with the arrival of a second group of immigrants.

2. The colony was laid out on the north bank of the Baraboi river, about 30 versts from Odessa. The steppe assigned to the colonists was rich grassland, with a layer of black humus about 8 vershok(1) deep and a sub-layer of yellow clay mixed with saltpeter and lime. The south bank, which has several lofty hills, provides the colony with some very fine building stone.

Since the population of the colony has more than doubled in the course of 42 years, it has become necessary, with the advent of the second generation, to plow the fields more often and to graze more cattle. As a consequence, the pastures are often bare, and the denuded soil is no longer as productive as it was in earlier years. Since land beyond the south bank of the river has a large gravel content, it is unsuited for grain and hay. However, near the village the colonists have planted vineyards and woods, wherever the stone quarries permitted such plantations. The trees are thriving quite well and in time can contribute to the enhancement of Freudental.

3. The colony of Freudental got its name from one of the first settlers, a certain Heinrich Herth, who reached this healthful eminence on the Baraboi river after his long and arduous journey.

4. In the beginning, only 36 families who had arrived from the Kingdom of Hungary were established here. However, since the government had intended to settle 78 families here and allotted 5,830 dessiatines to the colony (75 dess per family), 42 additional families from Hungary were directed here in 1807. At that time the land apportioned to Freudental exceeded that of any colony in the Liebental area. For that reason the colonists of Grossliebental lodged a complaint with the authorities and at a meeting convened in Grossliebental, the officials of Freudental agreed to accept the same quantity of land as the neighboring colonies. After a new survey was made, the land of Freudental was reduced, so that at the present it owns only 3,829 dessiatines, which means about 49 dess. for every farm proprietor.

5. Like most of the settlers, the immigrants from Hungary did not come here in organized groups, but independently and without any leaders.

6. The steppe which was assigned to these immigrants by Duc de Richelieu, who was at that time the Governor, was not inhabited when the settlers arrived. It was used by the Tatars as astureland for their flocks, and only a small part was cultivated. The colonists found only 20 unfinished dwellings, consisting of 4 wooden walls devoid of a roof.
(more is available at the link...)

Further Contacts on Huether

For further information see:

The Huether reunion in Wessington Springs, SD on Aug. 11, 2001 was a great success. It was decided to hold the next reunion on Aug. 9, 2003 at the 4-H Bldg. in Wessington Springs, SD again. We will start gathering at 10 A.M. again. For further info. contact us at richardsarah64@hotmail.com

Richard & Sarah Mittelstedt
726 Frank Ave. S.E.
Huron, SD 57350

Or the Website at www.huether.net

We have traced it back to Johann Ludwig Jacob Huether b. May 7, 1797 in Neu Verbes, Hungary and d. July 29, 1840 in Peterstal, Grossliebental, Ukraine, Russia. He married 1824 to Maria Barbara Margaretha Zechmeister b. May 28, 1800 and d. Oct. 13, 1852.

Germans immigrated to Hungary at this time before immigrating to Russia.

The library index site for the Nagels:
http://pixel.cs.vt.edu/library/libindex.html

The GEDCOM descendant charts are transcribed from the *Huether Family Tree 2004* by Sarah Mittelstedt.

www.ingramcontent.com/pod-product-compliance
Ingram Content Group UK Ltd.
Pitfield, Milton Keynes, MK11 3LW, UK
UKHW041948190726
13854UKWH00004B/1859

9 781304 735065